'Dear Mr S........,

I received a letter today from the Prison
Reform Trust saying that you would welcome
having someone with whom to exchange
letters. I'm afraid you've drawn my name out
of the hat.
It is Christopher.'

'Dear Christopher,

I did indeed receive your first letter. It was as
you said, how to start a correspondence with a
stranger.
About me? I'm fifty four, soon to be fifty five.
Born in Camberwell London; raised in
Scotland, in various homes; did National
service, (Royal Scots); married an american
girl at thirty nine; lived in Detroit for six and
half years; came home after divorce; got
drunk; got in a fight; eighteen weeks later
charged with Murder; pleaded guilty; got a life
sentence. "I'm not proud."
That's the hard part of the letter over. I can
breath out now.'

THE SHANNON TRUST

Invisible *Crying* Tree

TOM SHANNON &
CHRISTOPHER MORGAN

BLACK SWAN

INVISIBLE CRYING TREE
A BLACK SWAN BOOK : 0 552 14433 9

Originally published in Great Britain by Doubleday,
a division of Transworld Publishers Ltd

PRINTING HISTORY
Doubleday edition published 1996
Black Swan edition published 1997

The Publishers have made every effort to contact the owners of
illustrations reproduced in this book. Where they have been
unsuccessful they invite the copyright holder to contact them direct.

Cartoon by Graham Allen.

Set in Sabon by
Falcon Oast Graphic Art

Black Swan Books are published by Transworld Publishers Ltd,
61–63 Uxbridge Road, London W5 5SA,
in Australia by Transworld Publishers (Australia) Pty Ltd,
15–25 Helles Avenue, Moorebank, NSW 2170
and in New Zealand by Transworld Publishers (NZ) Ltd,
3 William Pickering Drive, Albany, Auckland.

Reproduced, printed and bound in Great Britain by
Cox & Wyman Ltd, Reading, Berks.

For Frederick William Shannon
and Thomas Michael Shannon.

I would like to thank several friends
who read Tom's letters and encouraged
me to seek a publisher, in particular
George Henderson, Evangeline and Tenniel Evans
and Christopher Spence.

CONTENTS

INTRODUCTION

Anyone's first thought of prison life must be of the boredom. The prisoner in this book begins with the phrase 'seven years of nullifying boredom'. Evelyn Waugh in *Decline and Fall* described the silence and the dull absurdity of it all. It makes the prison as a literary subject somewhat unattractive.

But is it really what prison is like? President Havel was imprisoned in Czechoslovakia in 1979. He wrote about it to his wife:

'*I used to think prison life must be endless boredom and monotony with nothing much to worry about except the basic problem of making the time pass quickly. But now I've discovered it's not like that. You have plenty of worries here all the time, and though they may seem "trivial" to the normal world, they are not at all trivial in the prison context. In fact you're always having to chase after something, hunt for something, keep an eye on something, fear for something, hold your ground against something, etc. It's a constant strain on the nerves, (someone is always twanging on them), exacerbated*

1

*by the fact that in many important instances you
cannot behave authentically and must keep your
real thoughts to yourself.'*

Mr Shannon, the prisoner here, is not as articulate as the President. But he is clear enough about the stress. 'I get lost in rage,' he writes. 'I have forty adjudications for fighting, wrecking cells, smashing machines, refusing work, attacking screws, and wrecking everything and anything. There's an awful shame and no forgetting in murder'.

On reflection, I believe Mr Shannon to be quite as articulate as the President, and a great deal more accurate as a guide than Evelyn Waugh. I commend this short book to anyone who does not know prison but wants to extend their knowledge of human nature.

His Honour Judge Stephen Tumim
HM Chief Inspector of Prisons

PROLOGUE

In the summer of 1992, I enrolled in a penfriend scheme that had been recently introduced by the Prison Reform Trust. Its object was to give prisoners a window on the outside world. I was allocated to Tom Shannon. These letters are the result.

I have not edited Tom's letters except where his grammar seriously disrupts his flow. I have also disguised the names of some officials.

My own letters, which I have been urged to include, are reconstructions. Since Tom gets so few letters, I felt I should take trouble over mine. I therefore always made preliminary notes and drafts which I kept in case he ever referred back to something in an earlier letter. I have tried not to cheat and improve on the originals but, since Tom did not keep them, I cannot be sure. They were probably longer and more full of waffle.

Otherwise, I think the letters speak for themselves. I do want to say, however, that neither Tom nor I will benefit financially if they make any money. He is not allowed to and I do not want to. A charity has been set up, to be known as the Shannon Trust, whose aims will be to help elderly lifers prepare for and cope with the 'out'. Such money as the book earns will be used to fund this trust.

ONE

FEELING OUR WAY

c/o Prison Reform Trust
59 Caledonian Road
N1 9BU

10th July 1992

Dear Mr Shannon   .

I received a letter today from the Prison Reform Trust saying that you would welcome having someone with whom to exchange letters. I'm afraid you've drawn my name out of the hat. It is Christopher. The Trust did not know your first name, only that you were Mr J. Shannon, 55 years old and liked reading and coarse fishing. Maybe they told you as much about me so I won't repeat it.

I suppose Shannon is Irish. The only other Shannon I have known was an Ulsterman, a really nice older colleague at work. He must be ancient now for I am 65. Someone on the radio this morning repeated that old saying that 'Youth is wonderful but wasted on the young.' Quite right. I am alarmed that my life seems to have slid by so fast, but I would not want to be young again – all that bashfulness and not knowing how to cope with girls. (I still don't but it doesn't really matter any more.)

I think I'd like to stay 65 but, of course, that's not allowed either. I guess, in your situation, you'd rather be almost any other age – before your troubles or after your release.

The Trust sent a bundle of pamphlets about life in gaol. All pretty depressing to read but not able to give a real feel of what it's like. Perhaps you'll be able to supply me with that. I don't think many people outside have much idea. The nearest I ever got to gaol was a staff dance at Strangeways. Thank God! I found that gloomy enough.

Can you get the books you want? What do you like to read? Can you get the peace and quiet you need for reading?

I mostly read history books but am at present ploughing through an incredibly badly written book on the 'Shining Path' – Peru's terrifying terrorist movement.

Do you like writing? I do and I think it works away anger to write about it. Let's try to help each other by writing then. I will look forward to hearing from you.

Yours sincerely
Christopher Morgan

25th August 1992

Dear Mr Shannon,

Back in July, I wrote to you at the suggestion of the Prison Reform Trust who said you wanted a penfriend outside gaol. I had a feeling that you might think you had drawn rather a short straw in me, an old bloke. I will quite understand if you want another dip in the bran tub again in case there's someone in there younger and prettier!

On the other hand, perhaps it's just the difficulty of starting to write to a stranger. I quite agree. I found it difficult. What seemed an amusing idea beforehand suddenly looks different when you've got to do it. Even so, I think you should have a go. The very fact that it's difficult makes it worth a try.

Anyway, here is another SAE. Please use it if only to tell me to piss off! Then I could go back to the bran tub.

Yours sincerely
Christopher Morgan

In replying to this letter, please write on the envelope:

Number . . . C61329 . . . Name . . . Shannon . . .

Medway Wing
H.M. Prison
County Road
Maidstone
Kent ME14 1UZ

[late August]

Dear Christopher,

I did indeed recieve your first letter. It was as you said, how to start a corresdence with a stranger.

After seven years of nullifying bourdom, well, Im off now as you can see. For you to bother a second time is good.

About me? Im fifty four, soon to be fifty five. Born in Camberwell London; raised in Scotland, in various homes; did National Service, [Royal Scots]; married an american girl at thirty nine; lived Detriot for six and half years; came home after divorce; got drunk; got in a fight; eighteen weeks later charged with Murder; pleaded guilty; got a life sentence. 'I'm not proud.'

That's the hard part of the letter over. I can breath out now.

When we inmates recieve a letter, our names are put on a letter board. An hour before I could get to the censors office, I knew I had a letter.

With comments like – 'Here Tom, you got a letter' – 'Caw who'd write to that old xxxx?' – 'Not a bird is it Tom?' 'No, it's from a man' I won't tell you what the next few comments where, you can gess.

It was nice, thank you. I'll have to owe you for the first stamp you sent. I sold it for a cigarette. Don't send any more

10

stamped envelopes. I get one second class letter free every week. I have hundreds in hand at the censor's office.

I hope this one finds you in good health.

The biggest battle in prison is lathergy. I have started a Gym routine to try and pull myself together. A P.T. officer has taught me to swim. I'm like a kid in the pool, makeing up for all the years I could not swim.

I'll have to go to the library for a book on how to write letters. I hope you can make sence of this one. 'There's no stopping me now I'v started.'

Anything you want to ask me about, me or prison life, feel free. It's nice to talk to someone,

Sorry about your first letter,

Yours Sincerly
T Shannon
TOM

c/o Prison Reform Trust
59 Caledonian Road
N1 9BU

2nd September 1992

Dear Tom,

I got your letter today and quite understand your hesitation. It was a very interesting letter. I don't think you need a book to teach you how to write.

I'm sorry I'm not the stuff fantasies are made of. I'm afraid I never was – never was propositioned even once in my life – and now I'm crumbly, red-faced with a purple nose, no doubt through alcohol. I'm not too proud either, especially of my nose and I've less excuse for drinking than you. I've had things much easier. It's just that I like the stuff and am surrounded by it – but I hate to feel drunk.

I'm so glad that you want to go ahead. I feel we could help each other but let's just see where it gets us. Let me start by telling you more about me.

I am a Scot – at least I support Scottish teams – but my father was a soldier and we lived all over the place. My first memories are of Buda-Pest. I was just too young to be in the war but was called up and decided to stay on because it seemed fun. I got out in 1964. I had travelled quite a lot – America, France, Germany, Arabia – but never saw (or should I say heard?) a shot fired in anger. I was rather sorry. I never found out if I could be brave or not. Probably just as well.

Then I went into the tobacco industry. A lot of people think that that's immoral but I think tobacco makes life a lot more bearable for a lot of people. I fear that if it's drummed out, people will just turn to something worse. I know I have had a lot of pleasure from tobacco.

12

For the last twenty odd years I've been farming too. When I left the army, I bought a little land which is run by a brilliant farm manager who does all the clever bits while I and my wife Ann pitch in when there's heavy work to be done and at weekends. There's not much money in it, but we've only once made a trading loss. We do beef cattle and cereals. It's a simple system, and we still have a lot of manual work because we don't have enough money to lock it up in new or sophisticated machinery.

I have four children, all grown up. The eldest is Stephanie, divorced with a son. The next is Andrew, married with two boys and working in Spain. Next comes David also married with a boy and a baby on the way. He's trying to develop a table importing business. Finally, Rupert lives in France with a girl friend and wants to write. Well, he does write but not yet enough to keep the wolf from the door. Luckily, his girl, Karin, earns a bit. Well – that's enough about me.

It must have been hard for you, breaking up in America. A happy marriage is the foundation of life for me but I think it is quite difficult to be married to a foreigner, even an American with the same language. Every nation has its own habits which can lead to misunderstandings – and there are enough of those in your average marriage anyway. You didn't say whether you had any children.

I take your point about boredom in prison. It must be soul-destroying. You must tell me if there's anything I could get for you that could help. In the meanwhile, just writing to each other will give us both an interest. Anything that helps me to understand your life now and before will interest me.

Yours ever,
Chris

PS Can you read my writing? Not everyone can (including me sometimes).

MEDWAY WING
H.M. PRISON
COUNTY ROAD
MAIDSTONE
KENT ME14 1UZ

25-9-92

Dear Chriss

If you ever take up crime, you wont go short of a drink. Sometimes the place is swimming in it. There are some cons who brew hooch, some for there own use, some for sale. I spent one evening drinking it in 1987, then spent the next week sitting on the toilet, so I give it a wide bearth.

You can also get brandy at twenty pounds a bottle, one of those flat half bottles, or whiskey, or gin.

You can also get canabis, or powder called scag. The cons who use scag are known as scagheads, very dangerious people. That's why I do a gym routine whenever I can. There are times when you have to defend yourself in these places. If you have to, you do it fast, hard, and vicious. 'I'm left alone'.

How does all this stuff get in? There's a vast population of screws, civies, to run these places, and vast profits to be made. So I will leave you to draw your own conclusions.

The money to pay for all these goodies is mainly smuggled in, in things known as chargers. A charger is any hollow cillinder type object that will fit inside a man's anus, plus many outher ingenious methods. Many cons go on home leave, or day release, to work in the local community. These are fixed termers. I'm doing life so I dont qulify for these priviligies. Ill tell you more in future letters or will run out of things to write.

14

So look out for the next thrilling instalment on prison life, your own soap opera on porridge eaters.

So Chriss, your the one that's clogging up my lungs with all these tobacco products. I work in the print shop here. I print, at the moment, these letters I'm writing on. I'm doing a run of one million wiche should be finished sometime after Xmas.

I am as I said, allowed one ordinary letter per week (see onvelope stamped O.L.). We can buy as many first class letter as we like from the canteen if we have the money. I earn £3.50 per week which I spend on tobacco. OLD HOLBORN costs £1.75 per half ounce. I buy hilton dark blend. £3.31 per two ounces, plus papers and matches. I had a pipe when I first came into prison. It was stolen, so I roll my own now. You can buy anything with tobacco. I just bought a pair of shorts from a con, for ½ ounce of old H.

'I'v just been unlocked, off to the Gym, more later.'
'Later and nackard'
The swimming pool is closed. One of the handicapped kids did a wet poop in it. The pool is small – ten cons and it is packed.

Our letters are not censored anymore. I will seal and post this one. A postman collects them every morning. Your letters to me are opened in front of me, just to see if there is any money in them. If so it goes into a private cash account. Your writing is fine. My mate two cells away is, or was a doctor so any words I don't get, he does. The library has a good supply of books I have read so many that they are a jumble in my mind. I do have two boys in U.S.A. 12–11 this year.

My x wife has married a man called Anson. She did send me two photos, through the Home Office, would you believe, but no address, so I don't know where they are now. I can only hope they dont know I'm in prison for murder. I hope it dosen't affect there lives. I told the education lady I have a pen friend. She says she will help me with spelling, and composition when there is a vacancy on her English class. I did a few years on farms, sheep farm in Tomintoul, Banffshire, and Balguider, and arrible farms in warwickshire during my itinerant youth and young manhood. So you and I have seen the change over from pitch fork and horse drawn binders to combine harvesters.

If we don't spoil our planet, there must be wonderful things to come. You are only ten years older than me. Look at the changes we have seen. Our grand children will be taken on holidays at butlins on the planet Zircon?

Yours Sincerly
T Shannon
TOM

P.S. As a farmer, you would cry if saw what the prison cooks did to your fine produce. (Wher's my stomach powder?)
TOM

c/o Prison Reform Trust
59 Caledonian Road
N1 9BU

1st October 1992

Dear Tom,

I found your letter when I got home. Thank you very much. Everything you say is new and a revelation to me. Life in gaol sounds pretty expensive, especially if you smoke or drink and considering what you can earn.

I have only drunk hooch once, in America. I was caught speeding in Virginia and they took me straight to the station to be judged. It was evening and the judge had to come from home and while we were waiting, they brought in a lorry full of moonshine. The police chief said he thought we ought to try it to make sure it was genuine and soon we were having a real party, which the judge joined as soon as he arrived. I can't remember what I was fined. I don't think I could remember next morning.

Gaol sounds bloody dangerous. I would have hoped that a tough reputation would have been a protection but if it just encourages them to try . . . ! Perhaps scag makes them reckless. (What is it made of – heroin? cocaine? Is it crack?) But it must be better to keep fit. What happens to those who don't?

Yes – the company I was in made roll-your-own tobaccos but not Hilton. That's a name I don't know, which just goes to show my ignorance even of my own trade. Or perhaps it is one of those niche brands aimed at a specialist market. Perhaps it's specially made for prisons. I gather from the Prison Reform Trust people that it is forbidden to send tobacco to a prisoner. Concerning money, why, if it can be sent in openly by post, do cons need to smuggle it in in chargers?

17

Things on the outside seem to be going on ok but I wish it was not so wet. Now is usually the best time of the year on the farm, with the harvest in and the anxious work done. Our hedges are cut, the winter corn is in and we should be enjoying a lovely Indian summer – but it is raining.

You are quite right. Although we don't have the latest kit, we've progressed beyond binders and hay-rakes. We've used a contractor's combine ever since we started. I can't think when I last saw a stook. (We called them 'shocks' where I grew up in the war.) Nowadays, we make much more silage than hay. Most of it goes into a big clamp, covered with a black butyl sheet. One of the great rituals of the year is the weighting down of this sheet with old tyres. They all have to be thrown up and spread out, two deep, by hand and as they are full of fetid rain water, we are soon all covered in stinking slime. It's not a job for the pompous, but we all think it's hilarious. We also put some silage in huge round bales which we wrap in butyl. You'd be amazed. I enclose a picture of some.

We sometimes bale straw in big bales if it's the only way to stop it getting wet. It saves time at harvest time but they are a problem to spread in the yard once the cattle are in. The technique is to unroll them but the steers think it's great fun to form a rugger scrum on the other side and roll them up again. It is possible to fool them by swapping sides but then they unroll the thing so fast that you can't guide them and, indeed, do well not to get trampled down in the rush.

When I see them cavorting around in the yard or lying on a sunny bank chewing the cud, I think – what a lovely life! Not a long one perhaps nor mentally stimulating, but blissful. I once calculated that it only takes four vegetarians to deny such a life to one animal since no-one can afford to raise animals if no-one will eat them. I respect vegetarians' choice, of course, but I resent it when they claim a higher moral ground than mine. I think they are actually rather selfish.

18

A million sheets of writing paper. That's difficult to envisage but it must mean an awful lot of letters. The Prison Reform Trust must have been hard at work.

Yours ever
Chris

In replying to this letter, please write on the envelope:

Number . . . C61329 . . . Name . . . SHANNON . . .

MEDWAY WING
H.M. PRISON
COUNTY ROAD
MAIDSTONE
KENT ME14 1UZ

7-10-92

Dear Chriss

I may have misslaid you about my earnings. £3.50 is my basic earnings. I can, if I attend every shift, and with quantity and quality of work, earn £6.25 max I manage £6.25 most weeks touch wood. I print letters, this one I am writing on now, is one that I printed. We say we are printing a million, because, we print letters then change to a different job then, back to letters. Everything we print goes to centrall prison-distribution somewhere in bedfordshire.

Scag is some perscent herion and some perscent garbage – talk, chalk, bakeing powder, whatever. It is habit forming. It is only when supply runs out that trouble starts, not too often.

Prison earnings go into our canteen earnings, credit account. Money comeing in from outside, from family, friends, goes into our private spends credit account. We are not allowed any cash in our possession, hence the chargers, to smuggle in cash, or powder, or canabis, or jewellery. Don't ask how bottles of booze get in. They do. You just put in your order to a fixer, hand over the cash and 'hay presto'.

Canteen spends can only be spent on canteen goods. There is a large selection. Private cash spends can be spent on, fruit, newspapers, mags, batteries, stamps, hobbies and all there relevent materials. Clothes, anything from catalogs, within reason. From all our prison earnings we pay 10p per week to the video Club.

This wing Medway has 174 inmates. There are four wings, 3 for common inmates, 1 Thanet for rule 43s, otherwise known as nounces. A nounce is a sex offender, and all that entails. Nounces are keeped on a special wing, to protect them from outher cons getting hold of them.

It is, at the time of writing 5.25 in the morning. I can here the night screws getting the kitchen workers up. The rest of us will be up at 7.45 – 8.20 breakfast – 9.00 work – 11.30 lunch – 12.00 midday bangup till 1.20PM. – then 2PM work, till 4.30 – dinner at 4.30 till 5 – 5PM bangup till 6PM – assosation till 8PM – then bangup till 7.45, next day. We have a sink and toilet in our cells. If you take one of those square lino tiles about 12″ square. My cell is 6½ tiles wide, 9 tiles long. About 12′ high, with bed and furniture. The poor swinging cat wouden't have a chance.

Well I should be getting the Farming news soon – here what you lads are groaning about now. I like that programme where the guy has his breakfast at a different farm all the time. An inmate who finished his sentence left me his radio. Is a tiny little sony, with ear stops. I'm afraid books take second place just now. I also purchased a THESAURUS for ½ ounce so my spelling should improve.

If you saw the food arriving here as a producer you would stand proud. If you saw it on the wing hotplate, you would weep. Something very mysterious happens to the food. The kitchen is run by inmates. The rate of changeover in kitchen inmates is enormous, so the food suffers. I'm lucky. My neighbours are mostly asian or nigerian or southamerican, so I get in on a curry or piella(?) now and then. We have a cooking area. You can order your food raw and cook it yourself. You can buy extra food or vitamins to supplyment your Diet, from your private cash spends.

21

Chriss I think you better get a note pad and start a gloss-ary of prison slang. I'm bound to slip in a word now and then but will try and explane its meaning. Now I'v started there's no stopping me, I'm a right little gossip, lots more to come.

Thank you for telling me what's happening on the farm. I'm getting to like this penfriendmanship

Your's Sincerly
T Shannon
TOM

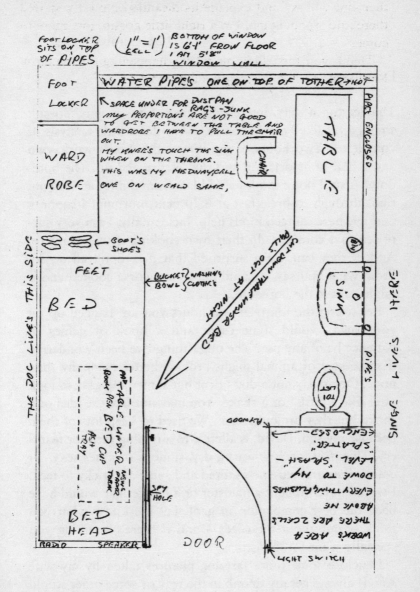

15th October 1992

Dear Tom,

Thanks for a very interesting letter. Life in gaol doesn't sound a bit like Porridge on the TV. I did a little analysis of your letter. Two hours of mealtimes, five hours work, two and a half of association and the rest banged up. The boredom! Also, I don't think I could last from dinner at 4.30 pm right through to breakfast at 8.20 next morning! I suppose that is where canteen funds help. Incidentally, I am very surprised that cons can do their own cooking if they want to. And, if they can, I am surprised that they don't all do so. From what you say, it could hardly be worse cooked and it might relieve the boredom.

Regarding the fourteen odd hours you are banged up on your own, would some cards and a book of games of patience be of any use? The other thing I've been wondering if some sort of animal might provide better company than none. Obviously not a dog or cat but something easy to look after like a bird – or a snake. You may not like the idea of a snake but they are quite nice. We used to keep lots of them because my son, David, is allergic to anything furry or feathery. They feel lovely – warm, dry, sinuous – rather sexy. Of course they are extremely stupid and some are tricky to feed. I would have thought a hamster or a budgerigar would have been the best companion in gaol. Let me know what you think – and about the cards – and if there's anything you specially want for Christmas.

I enclose some more farming pictures taken by my wife Ann [I always get my thumb in the way or some other stupid thing]. We must have many more, so I'll try and sort out a little tour of the farm for you.

Yesterday was a black day in the farm's year. It was the day we had to bring most of the cattle in from the fields. That means that from now on we have to feed them and bed them down daily. It's incredible how much ninety steers can eat – and how much shit they produce! It's drudgery but without it we could not enjoy that golden day in April when they go out again and spend the first moments of their liberty, joyfully galloping round their field.

I too listen to that farming programme on Sunday mornings. They have to resort to breakfasting with some pretty weird types. The trouble with farming today is that every normal crop is in over-supply. Farmers have been turning to exotic things like Evening Primroses and red deer but the limited demand for such things is soon sated. I fear it will soon be the same with the battle games and golf courses farmers are turning to. I am told that there are 7,000 golf courses now abuilding in England alone!

Still, we can't complain considering the subsidies we get. I feel ashamed when you think of what is happening to the miners. No-one is baling them out. Nor would they us if it wasn't for the French. It can't go on much longer. Europe can't afford it.

Yours ever,
Chris

TOM
NEW WING – WEALD WING
HM PRISON, COUNTY ROAD
MAIDSTONE

22-10-92

Dear Chriss,

Thank you for the pictures. I have put the wheat field, and
the combine harvester on my picture board. Views are the
right pictures for prisoners; you can wonder in them. The sky
is nice.

Story for you.
The God of thunder rode out one day,
Upon a snow white filly,
I'm thor he cried,
His horse replyed,
You forgot your thaddle thilly,

I hope you like this picture of my machine. Take away the
long hair from the skinny one, give him a heavy designer
stubble and that's me.

Do you like my new pad? I got fed up with those small
letters, so I made my own.

You once asked what happens to those that can't cope.
Death, by your own hand is the one everyone knows. There
are many deaths, of soul, sprite, will, and the slow death of
morals. Many of us, fall into a pit of gray darkness. Some
sink, some climb out. The climbing out is extremly difficult.
Some of us are helpless stumbling clowns, loaded with
regrett and remorse. The weight is tremendous, Some hide in
drugs. I got lost in rage, I have forty ajudications for fighting, wrecking cells, smashing machines, refusing work,
attacking screws, and wrecking everything and anything.
There's an awful shame and no forgeting in murder,

26

Someone was looking after me to send me down that road.

Joey:- a convict who is very heavy in debt, with a baron. He cleans for the baron, he washes the B's clothes, irons them, and may be of use in other ways(?). Any free time a joey has over, he spends doing favours for others for small pay,

Twenty five years in the army, you could think of a hundred ways for an all male society to degrade themselfs. Guilt is really something.

Your picture is of space. Do you have sheep or pigs, or chickens? I hope you have lots of Grand Children to whoop and shout. A farm without a child is a wonder going to waste. I was taken out of homes when I was thirteen, and put out to board with a farmer, outside Tomintoul Banffshire Scotland. God knows how I got to Scotland, when I was born in London.

I loved that farm, sheep, kai, hens, corn, spuds, neeps, tupping, peat, bees, home made cheese, oatmeal griddle cakes, pitch forks so full of hay, you looked like a walking haystack. I loved soup, potato soup, hare soup, and delicious pea and ham soup.

I grew up and discovered electric soup, and landed in hell's kitchen. Father Hugh Sinclare at Wormwood Scrubs, sends me playing cards.

Chriss, if you send me a Christmas Card, I will be more than happy. Things make you that little bit better than someone else,

I'v caused enough hurt.

We are not allowed animals of any kind. It would make the cockroaches very jealous,

We are allowed birds. I have to call them birds, I can't spell budgerigars (thesaurus). The longing on someone else's face, would lose me anything you sent,

My best friend is my sony; my second best friend is a printing machine. It gives me something to do. It took me nearly

27

seven years to get my radio. It was love at first sound. I rehearse and lead the Catholic quire, I like to sing, I'll tell you more about not copeing, (bit at a time).

Great exciting things going on here. Card phones installed, great queues and a lot of hello mums, a lot of tension gone, more smiles, outgoing calls only, two pounds for a phone card. They have already become trade goods, four for a sixteenth of canabis or three ounces of snout, or, four for a ten pound note, a bag of scak for the tenner. Take an aspirin, crush half of it and you have enough powder for a bag of scag. It's really a very tiny envelope, half the size of a postage stamp.

I bought a tin of Peaches this week, opened Sunday lunch time, did my oliver twist for more custard, then made pigs look polite, (scrumsious).

Your letters are diamonds. I hope the winter is kind to you and your's. Keep cosy. Do you fish? I have a card of a big carp on a strange shimmering card. It must be chinees. Fishing was my hobby on the out. Pike season coming up. Hope I leave you enough time to your farm work between these letters,

Keep or destroy the enclosed summary*. I have another one. It's how others see me, I hope it does not make you regrett writing to me. I'm not too nice a person, I am over twenty one physicaly. Mentally? Talking about that Scottish farm, I never once saw that hairless little monster, the Haggis, at least not off the plate, I saved a pound this week – another tin of peaches next week. 'Life is a gas'. Do my letters make sence? I'v rered this one. I don't know what to make of it. What do you think?

your's T. Shannon
TOM

---

*He enclosed the official report of his Lifer Review Board. Since it is a confidential and official document, I have paraphrased it.

LIFER REVIEW BOARD SUMMARY

As their sentence progresses, lifers begin to be reviewed periodically to evaluate their fitness for release and to consider what steps should be taken to prepare them for it. This is done by a Lifer Review Committee (LRC) chaired by one of the junior governors and including all those officials who should know the convict. Tom had had an LRC in 1991 and was due for a second in early 1993. The summary he sent me recorded a preliminary meeting held in advance of the formal review.

It starts with the basic facts about him including his 'tariff'. This, I subsequently discovered, is the recommendation made by the judge at his trial as to how long he should stay in prison. Tom's tariff had been 8 years.

There followed a summary of his prison career, which noted that he was 54 and had completed 6 years of his sentence. He had murdered a 79 year old man with whom he had lived for 13 years. Although he had admitted his guilt from the start, he refused to talk to Prison Service employees. He was therefore making little progress.

There follow a number of comments about him by officials and persons such as the prison chaplain, the psychologist and his outside probation officer. Between them, they note his good standard of work and keenness to learn. They are ambivalent about his social behaviour. He is polite and gets on with other inmates, but is a loner and 'can be difficult at times'.

The next section discussed his previous LRC. It noted his refusal to attend it or to trust anyone in the Prison Service, other than his outside probation officer. Full of remorse, he recognized alcohol's role in his crime. He had settled quite well into Maidstone but seemed to be unable to see a future for himself.

The report ends with the Board's recommendations. He should see a psychiatrist and be included in a Social Skills Course. Probation must encourage him to co-operate and persuade him that he has something to offer in life.

c/o Prison Reform Trust
59 Caledonian Road
N1 9BU

30th October 1992

Dear Tom,

Thank you for the letter. I will never again think of Thor in quite the same way. I like poems that poke fun at the great and the good – though I'm not sure Thor qualifies.

I very much enjoy your letters, partly I think because you are writing about the real problems of living up against harsh reality. Virtually everyone else I know, including myself, is to some extent cushioned from reality and can mould their world to some extent to their liking. The world's troubles are most unevenly distributed.

Are you sure that a bird would not help? Ann says budgerigars are highly entertaining and can be taught to speak. I think I'd prefer a mynah. They are hilarious but terribly noisy and would not do at all in a cell like yours.

I was rather impressed by the Lifer Review Board Summary. They are obviously trying hard to understand. Of course, even I can see that they are off target in your case but then you don't give them much help. I think that's a pity but at the same time I can absolutely understand how difficult it would be to share your innermost thoughts with some stranger, some screw, knowing that they will be discussed openly. I too have skeletons in my head which I don't want to talk about, even with Ann.

We sent a batch of cattle to market last week although they weren't as well finished as we like. If we were going to keep them, however, it meant worming them after which there is a month's embargo on sale – a sensible rule because we don't want to worm the unsuspecting public too. Nowadays, you

32

pour the worming fluid on their backs, having put on rubber gloves. It must be powerful stuff.

The cattle sold quite well and so we've bought some new young ones. Hideously expensive (average £420). We'll have to try hard not to lose any. For several years now, we seem to have lost one of our cattle to bloat, despite the care with which we inspect them daily. It is a new trend and I suspect it is related to the increased clover in our seed-mixtures. Clover is a gassy food but it also adds nitrogen to the soil, which saves on the fertilizer bill but not as much as a dead steer costs. Still, we feel that we're being very ecological.

You're right, you don't have too much room in your cell. Barely room to swing a budgerigar. God knows how they manage to squeeze two in. God knows how the two manage to avoid homicide.

Yours ever,
Chris

PS Instead of a budgerigar, here's a book of Gary Larsen cartoons. Not everyone finds him funny. I do. Do you?
PPS You could swing a cat in your cell if you did it vertically instead of horizontally.

C 61329 SHANNON
'LOOK' BACK ON—MEDWAY,
HM PRISON
MAIDSTONE
KENT

11-11-92

Dear Chriss

It was very kind of you to send me, the cartoon book. Thank you. I could not settle on Weald wing, so I'm back on Medway.

A good friend of mine was ghoasted out at five this evening. Ghoasted means taken from the wing, and put on a coach, in a taxi, or a prison van, and your gone, to another prison, no warning.

It takes a long time to make good friends. He was teaching me to play backgammon, 'Ah well.'

Did you see a small article in 9-11-91 sun newspaper, about Long Lartin prison? They did not even scratch the surface. I was there for two years, prior to comeing here. It was hell, pure hell. I'v been in segregation for three weeks, so your letter and book lifted my sprits down there.

Do you listen to classic, F.M.? It's beautiful.

An L.R.C. is a local review committee. It's like that summery, only more so. That's the one where you get your knockback. I am expectting a five year knockback, which means my next L.R.C. will be in 1997.

What do you think – here comes Christmass! I like Christmass, even in prison,

I'v got a couple of little skills. So I always make a few of my fellow inmates happy, with a few gifts ('small')

Someone gave me a poster of raging white water, in a forest. I stuck it on the roof, I can lay back and get lost, in it. (I think I told you?)

There is a youngster who is into weights, so I cut a picture

34

out of a colour mag, of a cartoon caracter, liften a bar with weights on the ends. I then glued it onto a piece of cloth, put two coats of varnish on it. I then had it sowen onto this kids jacket, I now have 27 stupid cutouts to do. I think I'v started a crase and why not!

I'm ducking in and out of different subjects in this letter.·

I'm not all I should be this time. My three week lock up has left me a bit shakey.

I feel like I'v driven a thousand miles, over a very rugged road, at 100 miles an hour. Still I'm behind my door now, so the world is at peace.

You say your Grandchildren like the garden. Don't grow elephant grass. They have it here, and it is full of rats. It's to be burnt down. We will all stand round with sticks and give these rats a pounding. 'Zut alors'

One day I was walking round the yard, when a conker, hit me from over the wall. I put it in the soil and put a plastic clear dome over it. The poor thing is gone dry, and dead.

I'm just listening to Itsack Pearlman and John Williams, Violin and Guitar. Life has its moments. Do you have a spare picture of a cow, like the ones in posh mags, about the best of breed, and stuff, but without the guy leading it? I have always coveted one of those pictures. I have two pictures of two sheep. They have white afro coats – must drive the sherers mad.

You can't beat the tough black face of the highlands. Sheep – what am I on about? Still, the vibrations above me tell me that not evcrone is thinking about sheep.

When I was in America, I stopped to speak to a farmer at a place just fifty miles north of Detriot. We became good friends, at Imley City.

He made a dam by wireing some spare tyres together, and letting natural silt comeing down streem fill them, and when they were full, lay some more on top. He had a good pool for ducks, and fish. Not a good idea while the grand kids are still so young.

In the future food may be so expensive, a few ducks, and

fish, for the table may be a bonus, I could give you a hundred tips on how to make porridge taste different, but, as you have never done me any harm, I won't, I dont envy you reading this one,

I dont know what to put on this last line!*

Well, that got rid of that line. I hope I find you in good health. Don't please, ever run your life down – first the army and then tobacco, and now a farm, and raised a family,

I'm proud to know you, Sir! Well, I'm taken myself off to whatever the gods have planned for me tonight. God bless you for now,

Yours sincerly
T Shannon
TOM

PS   I had a pet cockroach,
called harold
I just called him hal
He was, my many legged friend
My creepy crawley pal.
I kept him in a match box
underneath the bed
I stood on him this morning
poor old hal is dead.
I know Im going to miss him
for he was very nice,
now, I have two new friends,
a breeding pair of lice.
      T.S.
      copyright 1987

---

*Tom is obsessive about not wasting any of the page and many of his letters contain sentences and postscripts whose only purpose is to fill the last line. With the book's different pagination, it is not possible to duplicate his anxiety.

18th November 1992

Dear Tom,

Thank you for your letter and the picture of the fisherman. Ann and I have been arguing over how you made this. I say that it's a printed card which you've coloured; she says you've drawn it. Who's right? We both liked the poem about Hal very much. It is very sad – but very funny too. Got any more?

I thought it might amuse you to go on a walk round the farm so, the other day, when I set off on my rounds, I took a camera. Of course it had to piss with rain as you will see from the pictures. You will also see that I'm no great photographer! I have made a sketch map of the farm with a xxxxx line showing the track I followed. I have indicated each point from which I took a picture. I'm afraid the map is a bit wonky. The fields didn't seem to want to fit together quite right but it will give you an idea.

I thought it might be interesting to repeat this exercise from time to time so that you can follow the seasons and the changing patterns and rotations of the crops – and the wild things, too – the flowers and trees.

I'm afraid I don't have a picture of a cow right now. Actually we don't have cows – only steers. I'll try to find a nice one. In the meanwhile you'll have to make do with these few miserable sodden steers.

I am much intrigued by prison movements. Why were you sent from Medway wing to Weald? And why didn't it work out? What makes one wing or gaol preferable to another? And, most of all, why have you been locked up?

I am also in a muddle about your family. You've done six years in gaol and before that you lived with this bloke for was it 13 years? And yet you seem to have quite young sons in the States. It seems that it's a long time since you saw or heard of them. Do you think about them much?

I think I'd better stop this letter. Too many questions.

Yours ever
Chris

PS When you've fulfilled your order book for cut-outs, could you make one for my grandson, Thomas?
PPS What does 'tariff' mean? In the LRC Summary, they said yours was 8 years.

Reconstruction of my map of the farm.

xxx = my path

→ = direction of photos taken.

⌒ = hedgerows.

Dear Chriss

You would not believe the luck I'v been having over the last few days,

I told a screw about my mouth feeling like an ashtray, because my false teeth have taken a golden tan, due to heavy smokeing.

After lunch monday he gave me a large bottle of steradent, powder. Same day evening, a con was leaving on tuesday morn, came down and gave me a flask.

So here I am, one thirty, thursday morn, drinking tea, while my teeth are turning white in another cup. Marvelous init! If my luck keeps going like this, you never know, I might just trip over a ladder. I wont forget the badge for Thomas, (good name). I'v put a pounce out for some varnish.

My picture board is bursting with colour. Thank you so much. Even your map is up there. I tell visitors to my cell that the map was left to me by an old con, and his stolen money is buried somewhere along those xs.

I bound to find some idiot who will believe it. The pictures are lovely, real good.

The lad with the flask, also gave me a nice bed cover, with a curtain to match. Gee whiss, or is it wiss, or wizz

There's a bet on here. Are the black cows Aberdeen-Charoley crosses, or just Aberdeen? There is ¼ ounce of snout on it, so I would be glad if they were crosses. Maybe that's cheating? Second cup of tea just been poured, Aint life grand.

I was down at the seg because ever since the sinks and toilets were put in, I cover my spy hole.

41

I don't like to walk to the shower unit as it is way up the wing. The cold draught is a bit much, with just a small prison towel round your waist. The unit is always full of steam, and it drips of the cealing, so any clothes you take up there get wet. So I strip of in the cell and wash down. Also I sit on the throne from time to time.

A lot of screws are young ladies. Some cons have even been done for flashing. Your generation and mine were raised different from the boys of today. Most cons are in there twentys, early thirties. A lot are muggers, rapists and petty thives. Being in prison dosen't change them. Be a bit uncausious and half your goods go missing. You have to make sure your door is banged up before you go anywhere.

Me, the doc, and a few others, have a neighbourhood watch, (would you believe it!) Doc and all like to go watch the video. I don't, so I sit and read on a bench the doc made, and watch ther wing prowlers. I go to thursday quire practice, and chaple on Sunday so they watch.

170 people on the wing, and every one a crook, God luv a duck, and half of them on skag or wiss, or canabis, (where's that ladder) or just out of tobacco because of . . .

They goast us because, then we dont have time to plan escape with outside help, en route. Most escapes happen en route, from prison to prison. Most escapes are not reported to the outside world.

A five year knockback is not so bad. The home sec says all life serving cons should serve 15 years. I'm almost half way, and after all Fred my victim is dead. How many years of his life did I rob him of? I deserve the sentence. Fred did not.

I have that picture I asked about. I found three Country Life in the chapel office and – hay presto. In fact, I have four pictures one of a shire horse.

I heard the vicar (C. of E. vicar) ask, if anyone had seen some Country Life mags. I can look so innocent at times, and there I am on about petty thives.

Thats another sin I'll have to confess to Fra Dennis. Hope he dosen't burst out laughing like he did when I confessed about mars bars that went from the canteen.

I just don't know what tariff means. I always thought it was another name for a menu.

Old lags do disappear suddenly.

I think I'll become a vegetarian.

Lord, you don't think I'll be a stew in 8 years?

It's almost 4 oclock. Sleep I think. More tomorrow nite. I write these on my knees in bed, hence, terrible writing, I have to have a blanket round my shoulder – cold, cold cells. I better get that sleep. I hate putting the light out. The dark mingles with my conchence, scares me. Childish, what do you think? Some tough guy! Sleep!

How do I do those cards? You find a cartoon, in the Mirror or the Sun or a mag. Devide it into squares ¼″. Mark a piece of tracing paper same number of squares, light (same size as card you will use). Enlarge bit of cartoon you want. When satisfied, go over enlarged tracing paper with heavy pencil.

Then turn the tracing upside down on card. Go round tracing with blunt stick or empty biro. Colour with short strokes, like so *wwwwwwwwwwwww* only neater. Then edge with fine *wwwwwwwwwwwww* point pen.

I will send you a bottle of hooch, copied from advert. This one just cut out the bottle that was depicted, drew round it and coloured – stuck bottle on piece of card first, to stifen. Will send card and bottle, then you will see. You will need felt tip pens, fine point pen. You will not need much practice, as I still have your pen drawing of hay bales, the round ones. Very good. Look forward to your first home made card. Have another look at my card. You will see what I mean. Feel the back of the drawing. It's cheaper than buying them. How much do cards cost?

I also make frames from scraps, from book binders shop. Your wheat field is in one of them.

Our phone cards have, FOR USE IN H.M. PRISONS ONLY, on them, so a asian here collects the used ones, sends them to his brother who sticks them together, back to back, drills a hole in them, puts them on key rings, and sells them as key fobs.

I had a brother who died age four, Michael. I named my second son in States after him.

6-45 THURSDAY MORN, The curtain is not a good idea, makes the cell too black.

I'll have to tell you the saga of short planks and the pigeon. It's a true story. I almost roll about my cell laughing about it sometimes.

Also I'll tell you about Long Lartin, but it will take so long. I'll have to slip in an extra letter. If our letters are too heavey, ozs that is, then we are told to lighten them.

We are to be banged up till eleven this morning for wing spin.

Don't you think it is the height of stupidity, to give us warning if there idea is to find contraband?

Good job I haven't put down my xmas hooch yet. I'v been promised a small sachet of brewers' ycast, so if I dont get a spin between now and xmas eve, cheers!

I'll be even more lucky if me and the doc can get a $\frac{1}{16}$th of puff as well. I'v had two brews, and two $\frac{1}{16}$ths this year. Once for my birthday in feb, and doc's birthday in june.

The trick is to go to xmas mass, then come back to bed and sleep all the rest of xmas day, so you stay awake all of xmas night.

Wish I'd kept some of that hot water for now. Cup of tea would be nice now. Ah well soon be eight oclock. Do you notice more spaces? Should make it easer for you to read.

Thank you for the lovely pictures again. Your a champion. Amen.

till again, yours
T Shannon
TOM

SEE OVER LEAF FANCY EH

44

WING WISPERS, OR, NUDGE NUDGE

See him over there,
he's a ponce,
The one he's talking to,
he's a nonce,
See that one there,
dont know what he did,
they, say its something,
to do with kids,
see the one beside him,
he'll do more than life,
should have heard,
what he did to his wife
see him over there,
he's I.R.A.
never getting out,
no way,
What do you mean?
What have I done?
Im innocent
ask anyone,

c/o Prison Reform Trust
59 Caledonian Road
N1 9BU

30 November 1992

Dear Tom,

I'm glad things are going so well. That screw with the Steradent bottle goes a long way to restoring one's faith in human nature.

I feel for you about your teeth. I've recently been in trouble too. My top teeth eventually got so loose they had to be wired together and moored to the one sound one on each side. Then, one day last year, I collided with a bullock. He knocked the right hand one adrift and so that the whole structure took on a list of about thirty degrees. Hating the whole idea of false teeth, I carried on like that for a bit, eating bread and milk and frightening the horses, but eventually, the whole lot had to go – early one morning.

It only took a day to get a temporary top plate made but it was the longest and most humiliating day of my life. My mouth felt like it was filled with a clammy plastic balloon which I suppose was my upper lip sucked into the vacuum. God knows what I looked like. I decided to take refuge in the British Library but on the way there, a Jap tourist stopped me.

'Legion Slee?' he asked.

'Oo-air?'

'Legion Slee!' he repeated rather petulantly. Clearly suspecting he'd picked on a half-wit, he showed me his map.

'Aah!' I said, 'Oowee'un Fwee'

I took him by the shoulder and propelled him silently to Oxford Circus.

'Air', I said, pointing southwards, 'Oowee'un Fwee.'

I won't bore you with more of that day's miseries. All I can say is that by 5.00pm, I was completely reconciled with the idea of a top plate. Mind you, it was some weeks before I got the damned thing under control. It felt like some flying saucer trapped in my mouth and trying to get out.

I'm afraid those weren't Angus-Charolais cattle in the photo. They were Friesian/Limousin crosses. I doubt if such things existed when you went into gaol. Continental breeds have more or less wiped out the old British ones, although we do occasionally get Angus still. I don't know when I last saw a Shorthorn and even the Hereford is getting rare.

Limos are very wild. The other day, we brought that lot from the photo in for the winter. Where the council road turns into our yard, its colour changes from black to grey and they thought this looked really dangerous. For twenty minutes they refused to cross it and we had to call up reinforcements in the end. Luckily no car came down in the lane, otherwise they'd have probably set off back to Limoges. We had a huge limo last year that was particularly impossible. When the lorry arrived to take him to market with half a dozen others, we built up the barriers round the loading bay to about eight foot high (two five bar gates strapped one on top of the other.) He just sauntered up to one and cleared it from a standstill! We managed to get him back again and, this time, he decided to escape from us by rushing into the lorry. You can imagine with what speed we got its ramp up!

The rain hasn't stopped for days and the farm feels as if it is slowly trickling downhill. I hope it's not. In a way this suits me because I've got my book back from the publishers marked '3 out of 10 – can do better.' So I've got to stay indoors and rewrite all the bits they don't like. That's easier if it's raining.

Ann and I were both wrong about how you made that card. It's clever. We liked Wing Wispers very much. Keep them coming. I think your poems are very good.

Yours ever,
Chris

TWO

THE STANLEY KNIFE

8-12-92

Dear Chriss

Thiss has to be my last letter, It's been a pleasure.

I should be gone by the time you get this, to the Island or Dartmoor. Who cares? A prison is a prison. All the view I ever have is a wall. Hence the hope of falling over a ladder. When I move to another prison all my goods fit in a plastic bag.

This time I'll take my thesaurus, come and brush, pen, and two personal towels, and pictures, papers. I wont be able to take radio, or any of the things given to me by other inmates, as these were not on my property card, when I entered this place. 'Rules are Rules.'

I'm on Segragation 'again'! Another hard and bloody punch up, with 3 twenty one year olds, who stole the blades from my work stanley knife.

I was nicked, fined four pounds.

You see Chriss, you can't say the truth of what happened, when on ajudication. That would be grassing others up.

A grass in any prison is looked on as something lower than whatever.

So you keep quiet, take the punishment, and settle it in your own way.

The youngsters were warned what would be the outcome, giggle, giggle. What that old cunt? Whose gonna worry about him?

One's in hospital, two are bruised, and my right fist is swollen, and I'm off and down a few regresive steps. 'So be it'.

If and when I return to this area, I will ask penfriends if you are still around.

I could keep in touch, from whatever 'cat A' prison I'm

sent to, but it takes all one's powers of survival to live in those places. The end of the day leaves the nerves so taut that you jerk and jive as you unwind, towards sleep.

The first rattle of the keys in the morning brings the fear. The wrong word, the look, a misconstrued jester, and your gore becomes part of the decor.

In every prison there are segregation units, hospital units. In all these units there are strip cells with straight jackets waiting. They are used very often.

Also padded cells, and the liquid cosh.

Thats why its always best to fight.

It was horrible having to go for those youngsters. They have not long arrived from a young offender's prison.

They have learnt a valuable lesson, but cost me a few more years. My LRC knockback will be more than five years now.

I'm in for murder, a blade has gone missing, what must that look like on my sheet.

It's so safe, so secure, so peacefull here on the segragation unit.

There are 578 bricks in the wall I stare at, a large number of names of the Killroy Woz Ear type, a great variety of food stains.

A pisspot in the corner, with the smell of all those who have missed it for the last 100 years. A bed bolted to the floor with D brackets, a cardboard table and chair. You can tell how long some people have been in the cell by the groups of scratch fives. 1111 1111 11 = 12. I been here 1111 1 six days.

When you live in a cell with just a pisspot, you keep a couple of newspapers under the bed, in case you need a shit.

Then you throw the shit parcel out of the window, its better than living with your own stink.

Not every thing is bad. Being down here has saved me a ½ ounce. I lost the bet. No luck for the wicked.

All the femail screws I'v met have been charming, good to talk to, easy going, some very good to look at. We need more of them. They have a calming effect.

But, if you heard the way some of the cons talk to them –
'good God'.

I saw a programme once, where a policeman said 80% of
the people were good, 20% were animals, and he spent 20%
of his time with the good, and 80% with the bad.

In prison you spend 90% of your time with the bad, and
10% with the good.

You can meet a great guy today. Tomorrow he'll split your face.

I cant talk about Fred, yet. He still haunts me. He was
Fredrick William Bradbury.

My first son is Fredrick William Shannon.

When I come back from the lower part of hell I'm going
to, my pen will seek you out.

Till then my friend wish me sanity.

Yours sincerly
T Shannon
TOM

P.S. Get that book done
Good luck with it.

THE FIRE
Alfonce Pious Magguire
Set his cell on fire,
Off he was led,
to the seg,
opps, tripped,
split his head,
as he took
that assisted fall,
he left some teeth
on the wall,
dont feel sorry
for Alfonce,
I beg,

dont give a hoot,
the nasty little lire
swear's, the wall
was an officer's boot.
1988

PS The God of Thunder is not mine, I found it in a colledge
rag.

CHRISTOPHER
My friend Chriss,
is a farmer,
I dont know,
were at,
e milk's is cow,
every morn,
give's some to,
is cat.
is farm, is worked
by a manager,
is kitchen, is run
by Ann,
he sends me,
pictures and letters,
Happy is what,
I am,
I hope e takes
this ode,
plants it in,
the ground,
perhaps in time,
to come
a poem tree,
will be found,
8-12-92

c/o Prison Reform Trust
59 Caledonian Road
N1 9BU

15th December 1992

Dear Tom

It seems a long time since I heard from you. I hope there's nothing gone wrong for you. I expect it's just the Christmas post snarling everything up so I'd better get this off without any further delay – to wish you a Happy Christmas and many more of them.

I suppose even in gaol there is some attempt to make Christmas a little different from other days.

We'll give the cattle an extra bit of bedding on Christmas morning. Ann and I will have them for company, and of course each other which is bliss. The children are all too widely scattered to make it the sort of family gathering I remember as a boy, with all the aunts, uncles and cousins out in force. Mind you, I'm not complaining. We usually ended Christmas hating our cousins and in a sulk, which it would take most of the year to get over.

Let's hope you end the day in a good mood!

Yours ever,
Chris

PS Before I had time to post this, your letter of 8th December arrived with news of your move. First – I'll be really sorry if it means the end of our letter writing. I have enjoyed it very much – and learned a great deal too. Why can't we continue from whatever gaol you are sent to? Even in the worst of them, you would have moments of calm when you could write, even if only a couple of lines.

Furthermore, if you lose your radio, that would be awful.

A gaol without music strikes me as terrible – even more terrible. If you do lose it, I would like to send you a Walkman. I suppose one with earphones would be best. I could get a combined one with radio and tape player, if you like. Let me know.

But most of all, I'm horrified by this business of the Stanley knife. Given all its implications, maybe it would be better for you to be ghosted when you come out of seg. When you know where it is, please let me know. I really don't want us to lose touch and even the most horrible gaol could be made better by an occasional letter. So I will be waiting through Christmas for some news of you – with a lot of anxiety.

PPS Thank you very much for the two poems. I wish I could plant an ode tree. At least there's not an ode mountain in the EEC. Anyway – HAPPY CHRISTMAS, wherever you are!

Dear Chriss

I'm still here, all inter prison movements have been stopped.
So I wait and wait.

A wing governor came to see me, to tell me I have an
L.R.C. in february. I hope to god I'm not here till then, at
least not on seg.

I still have my radio. It wont be confiscated until I go
through reception, on my way out to some other nick. Some
of the lads here say that if a decent screw is on duty, I could
get my sony through. I can only hope.

It's midday here on Christmas day. I went to mass at 9o'c
– no organ player. It's hard to sing without music but we got
there. As I had not had anything to drink, I now have a soar
throat.

We are allowed any kind of radios. Some of the youngsters
(most) have ghetto blasters, with twin speakers, twin tape
things and disc things. A lot of cons have tape machines,
with amps and speakers. Some of the speakers are as big as
suitcases.

This causes a lot of rows, sometimes punch ups. The noise
can be terrific, but after ten at night, you have to tone down
the noise, or listen through head stops. Most cons comply.
Now and again you get a drug user who falls asleep, so the
screws have to go in and deal with it. That's a nicking.

I got a base ball cap from my propation lady in
Birmingham, that will keep the sun out of my eyes, when I
play in goal for the over fiftys.

If I do lose my sony, I will take up on your very generious
offer. A decent radio with good sound repro, is a dream, and

tapes too. Well tickle me pink, that would be something. You might find it hard to believe, I do spend a lot of time dancing in my cell, a sort of whirling dervish dance, I think it keeps me fit. What do you think?

I have calmed down since my punch up. One of the kids sent me a note of appology with a half ounce of snout. 'What a nice gesture'.

I just had a cup of mushroom soup and a Christmas duff – 'yummy'.

I'm a vegetarian, not that I don't like meat. I think with all the bang up meat can lie very heavy on your tum, so I eat light. I was well over 15 stone in 86, now I'm just under 10 stone.

So how can a skinny old Boy like me take on three 21 year olds and other assorted lumps. I'm a tenacious old B.stard.

Do you like the spaces? Your letters are showen me how to write mine.

Young Noreen came to live in England, sending her Mum £20 a week.

The mother wrote thanking her, and could she, Noreen, send a bit more?

So young Noreen sent her Mom £50 a week. Mum wrote back, saying that dad had lost his job.

So young Noreen sent £100 a week.

Christmas eve, mum came to England to see Noreen.

Noreen, said Mum, where do you get all your money?

Noreen told her.

Mum fainted.

When Mum was revived, she said, Noreen, tell again.

Noreen told her.

O, thank god for that, said mum, I thought you said you turned Prodestant.

I will keep writing, I keep asking the screws is there any letters. I think I become a letter addict. Thank you for the card. I like it.

Did you hear Judge Tumim, talking about Long Lartin. He vindicates everything I say. The devil thrives yonder. A lot of cons at Long Lartin are doing bird for murderious robbries, and other acts of greed. Putting them in prison dosen't stop this greed. These socalled gangsters live very high on the hog with there ill gotten gains.

I'll have to write and tell you about the gangster system.

It's they, the gangsters, who run the under culture of any prison.

Well, it's 1-30 xmas day, slop out soon. No sinks or toilets in seg cells, just a piss pot. If you want a crap, you have to do it in a couple of sheets of news paper, then throw it out the window. Outher wise your cell can stink something horrible.

Ther's only two other boys on the seg with me. About every couple of hours one of them goes apeshit, smashing his cell and screaming.

I think he's a drug addict, needing a fix. When he quiets they will take him to the hospital unit.

I heard at church that a few lads were nicked last eve – drunk and dissordly, would adam and eve it!

Well I'm off, as I'm board stiff I will write the gangster senario and send it to you.

For Now, Good luck, God bless

T Shannon
TOM

TOM SHANNON
MEDWAY MAIDSTONE
KENT

29-12-92

Dear Chriss

You must be thinking a letter bomb has exploded over you. I had to get this one out to you to let you know. Everything is back to normal, without any repercussions, I hope.

A most remarkable turn of events. You remember the noted, half ounce apology? The same kid found the stanley knife blade under my work table.

It is one of these remarkable animated stanley knifes. What happened was this, 'ahem'. The knife unscrewed itself, dumped the blade under my work table, then rescrewed itself together again. My own fault really. I placed it too close to my spinage sandwich.

I think the kid was got at, to hand in the blade. I have written a statement to that fact, (that it was handed in).

My sheet is clean, my fine returned, back on the wing 'like what happened man'. Thank god, my sony is safe till I am moved, which should be a long time from now. Old dock was in a happy mood when I returned to the wing. I'm happy too, everything is hunky dory. Till the next time, 'O LOR' I have sent a prison newspaper. I hope you find it interesting.

I don't know if two letters to the same address will be allowed in one week. There's only one way to find out.

I am compleatly wrung out, toatally lathargic. I will close down and give you time to catch up with this lot.

I think you are right about keeping an outside contact. It helps.

Thank you for being there, for hearing my bleets, my invisible crying tree.

T Shannon
TOM

(quiver of fright)
If I should live,
a hundred years
and more again,
wish I would,
none like these,
I have lived,
would be,
so filled,
with pain,
hear you
the crys,
of small boys
raised among sticks and straps
of charity,
see you

The tears
in eyes
filled with hate,
of nuns,
uniforms of
evil black,
here again
these uniforms,
are back
cold and dull
segregated cell
womb of daylight,
hell of night,
rattle of keys,
quiver of fright

20-12-92
T Shannon

MY TWO NEW FRIENDS

That breeding pair of lice
whom I said,
where very nice,
got somewhat,
out of hand,
when starting
to expand,
They started on my head
spread all over the bed,
They got in nooks,
and crannies,
I never knew, I had
the daily
jittering and jiving
almost drove me mad,
I had to shave my head
I had to burn the bed,
I painted my body
With iodine,
now all the lice
are dead,
With the telling
of this story
My throat
is thick.
wait,
O LOR, O NO,
I got another
itch,

25-12-92
T.S.

PRISON GANGSTERS OR PARASITES

Dear Chriss

What is a prison Gangster? Invariably he is a Londoner. That's because of London's fast population, so the majority of cons are Londoners.

I have met a Welsh Baron-Gangster (black) and a south American, Italian, Jocks and Geordies. But the vast majority of Baron-Gangsters are Londoners. You would be hard put to seperate a baron from a gangster.

A real gangster, the old fashioned type that came into the system with there reputations, are a dead or dying breed. They ruled there manors on thc out, usualy in the east end of london. Such as the Crays, though I would say the Crays were part old type gangster, and part of the new vicious type ruled by greed.

A prison Gangster's only reason for being, is to live off the mugs. If you were standing on a prison landing, with a click of these gangsters, you would here one of them say, as the rest of us were making our way to work;- 'Look, there they go, the mugs, the fucking mugs.' They have a repetitive turn of phase like fowl mouthed parrots.

Whereas you can buy drugs and other commoditys from the drug barons, gangsters do sell, or deal in drugs, but there main objective is apperences. They put a lot of time and effort into looking the business. They will come out of there cells looking scrubed and polished, shirts ironed, every crease in its proper place.

They will walk the leanth of the wing. If you want to curry favour with them, you say as they pass;- 'Hay Joe, cor, you look the business!' He will stop for a minute or two to let you see his sartorial splendour, saying something like;- 'I do fink it wofe tikeing time to dwess propa.' As he moves on to seek more compliments, you turn to your mate and say;- 'What a fucking pillick.'

They walk about in what they think is an all knowing silence, but when they do talk they want everyone to here them. There banal utterences usualy start with;- 'Here, here mate, wot ya fink, ah was arskin a screw? here mate, ow cum, a man like, ow cum, ma mate got goasted? no wot e said?'

'No Joe, what did he say?'

'e said, a mean like, e said, don arst me, don arst me. I arst you, ah mean like e's a pissing screw! if e don no oo does?'

They do for some reason get all the cushy jobs, like wing cleaners, and pay some joey to do there work. Say a wing cleaner gets £4 a week, they will give a joey £2 A WEEK or they will keep the £4 and slip the joey a bit of canabis, or if the joey is in debt to them, the poor sod gets nowt.

When out on the sports field, watching football they stand around in small mobs, trying to outshout each other with things like; 'here ref where's your glasses?' They will all fall about laughing at each outhers shouts, saying;- 'cor nice one arry!' The fact that arry shouts the same thing two or three times per match, and has been doing so for the last ten years is nither here nor there. He will still shout next week, they will still fall about laughing. 'nice one arry!'

Very few of them have spent much time outside prison. You here them talk about young prisoner jails, as other people talk about countrys they've been to.

There is another kind of gangster, the cardboard cut-outs or would be gangsters. These are muggers or petty burglers, or even rent boys, who try to pass them selfs off as something they are not. I haven't met a cardboard cut-out who did earn less than hundred thousand on the out, and yet they are always on the pounce (begging). Yet these cut-outs are the most dangerious in as much, as the other gangsters use them to do there dirty work. These cut-outs are so keen to be seen as up and comeing boys, that they do pay homage to the made up gangsters.

If a made up gangster has a grudge against me, say, he will call up two or three of these cut-outs, then after a bit of drug payment, send them after me, with instructions to do him some damage. As luck would have it I have not had any trouble with gangsters. I have seen some of the results of these cowardly attacks, not nice.

They, the gangsters, invariably get the red bands, (trustees) – 'andy for ducking and diving, mate.' They are always adressed as Tom, Joe, Bill, by the screws. The rest of us are Shannon this or Shannon that.

You will find the gangsters frolicking in the gym every afternoon. The rest of us, the mugs, are in the sweat shops.

Well chriss thats gangsters, with some jelousy. They do have a good life compared with the rest of us. They do rule the roost. We mugs do toe the line, or get damaged.

Zut Alors
MOM AMIE
T Shannon
TOM

P.S. Chriss, dont feel you have to answer this letter. Im just
BORED

c/o Prison Reform Trust
59 Caledonian Road
N1 9BU

5th January 1993

Dear Tom,

Please forgive me for not writing sooner but Christmas and its aftermath is always a busy time. It's when I finish the farm accounts and that sort of thing. They are pretty simple accounts – or would be if I could add them up properly. I do them on a little computer nowadays which in theory adds them up for me but I still manage to cock it up. Rubbish in, rubbish out, as they say. I always seem to make some fool error. And then I've been hard at it on my book.

Anyway, it was great to get three of your letters all together. Happily, I read them in the right order. I started with the troubles with the stolen blades, the fights, seg and the rest and would have been sleepless had I not been able to carry through to the happy ending. What a story! What a drama! But, thank goodness, a happy ending. But, my God, what a dangerous life it is! I didn't watch all the episodes of Porridge but they were clearly very misleading – a heart-warming tale of ordinary prison folk. Someone ought to write a soap about prison as it really is.

Since I started this, your letter about the baron-gangster system has arrived which had Ann and me holding our sides. Mind you they are funny to read about when written up like that but clearly they are vicious and dangerous. Otherwise they would never get away with it. I suppose the other thing is their alliance with the screws. According to his report, Judge Tumim agrees with you that Long Lartin is virtually run by the gangster-barons.

Going back to the knife business, you must be incredibly fit and resolute to have defeated those three young men – and done them such damage. I suppose fifteen stone distilled down to ten has left you wire and muscle. And then, I guess you learn some self-defence in a life like yours. Still, I'm lost in wonder.

Thanks for the two poems. I liked them both very much – and felt very flattered. No-one's ever written a poem about me before – or any prose for that matter! But I feel sorry for your pets. They all seem to come to sad ends. Perhaps I'll forget about that budgerigar idea.

I'm appalled at the idea of all those ghetto-blasters going. It must be hell on earth. I think that I should send you some earphones. They would help you shut the noise out and hear your own music too. But could you dance in them? Let me know if they would be useful. Also, I have a calendar with pictures of cart-horses. Shall I send that too?

I too sometimes dance about when I think I'm alone and go crimson if someone walks in. It's the same with singing – or the droning noise I call singing. I like to do it but the only time I can let myself rip is inside the cab of a tractor out on a distant field. I'm very jealous of your ability to sing.

Tell me more about sports in gaol. I used to be a goal-keeper too. I loved soccer and can remember wondering what could be the point of living once one got too old to play it. It didn't take me long to find out. Later when the boys were young we rigged up a goal on the lawn so that I could show them my amazing skills but the ground seemed to have got much harder. I found I could no longer dive for the ball to save my life.

It's been bitterly cold outside. I hope they keep Maidstone gaol reasonably heated.

Yours ever,
Chris

PS HAPPY NEW YEAR!

THREE

THE SHIVE

c/o Prison Reform Trust
59 Caledonian Road
N1 9BU

25th January 1993

Dear Tom,

I began to have an uneasy feeling that it was a long time since I last heard from you – at least, longer than usual. So I looked back and found that the last letters were those three about the lively Stanley knife. The last one was dated 29th December, so I suppose it's not so long really. Letters sometimes take ages getting here via the Prison Reform Trust. I expect there's one on the way already.

I suppose the reason I started to worry was the possibility that you'd been ghosted, as you were expecting. I suppose it is even more likely because of the fights you have been in. Although you were completely vindicated, the screws may be afraid that it could break out again. What I could not understand is why you thought that, if you were ghosted, our correspondence would have to end. You did not explain why and I don't agree at all. I would like to go on with it.

Having started to worry, I thought I might as well write anyway, without waiting for one from you to arrive, especially as I need to know:-

[a] whether you want that calendar

[b] whether you would like some ear-phones

Maybe if you've been ghosted, you've lost your radio too. If so let me know at once. I can't remember who but someone once said; – 'He who hears music, finds his solitude peopled.' – or something like that.

There isn't much news from here. One curious thing is the price of fat cattle. Under the new Common Agricultural Policy of the Common Market, we are to receive much bigger subsidies to offset the drop in prices. The subsidy increase in our case will be from about £2,500 a year to at least £12,500! At the same time, to everyone's surprise, cattle prices have gone up sharply. If it goes on like this we'll make a killing. It can't last. I think it was the ancient Greek, Euripides, who first said; 'Whom the Gods would destroy, they first make mad.' I'm expecting a thunderbolt to land on the Agricultural Bureau in Brussels any day now (hopefully with a second one on the Ministry of Agriculture.)

Hope to hear from you soon – from wherever you are.

Yours ever,
Chris

PS I seem to be full of quotes today. Sorry about that.

c/o Prison Reform Trust
59 Caledonian Road
N1 9BU

10th February 1993

Dear Tom,

Another two weeks and nothing from you. I really am beginning to worry. Is it something I said? Or are you in some sort of trouble? (OK – I know you're in trouble but I mean especial, new trouble) I feel something must be wrong. I enclose a stamped envelope. Just one sentence would do.

In the meanwhile I still have no very exciting news. Winter is an endless round of bedding and feeding the cattle and one measures the passage of time by how far the face of the silage clamp has receded. But wait! I do have news! I have sent off the final chapter of my book, duly revised and, I hope, ready for the printers. I can't tell you how happy I am to see it go. If I have to revise it once more, I think I'll have a nervous breakdown. And yet I fear I may miss it. It has been such a large part of my life for the last few years.

Please let me know what's happening.

Yours ever,
Chris

c/o Prison Reform Trust
59 Caledonian Road
N1 9BU

22nd February 1993

Dear Tom,

Now I really am worried. I rang the Prison Reform Trust to ask where you were and they have just come back to me to say that you are still in Maidstone. I fear something has gone wrong.

It is now six weeks since I heard from you and nearly two months since you last wrote. Perhaps you want to stop all this letter-writing. If so, you might have let me know! I'll be really sorry if you want to stop. I have been finding your letters very entertaining – well, more than that – always interesting, often very funny and sometimes moving and sad. If you want to stop, I fear I won't find another con who can write so well.

But my worry is that it is not just that you want to stop. I am afraid something worse has happened which is preventing you. Whatever it is, please let me know. To demonstrate how serious I am, I am investing in yet another stamped and addressed envelope. So you have no excuse.

Yours ever,
Chris

18-2-93

Dear Chriss

I am, and have been ill, something inside my abdomen,
I lost a lot of stuff out off there sometime ago.
I got a scar from my sternum, to just above my daintis.
The pain can be severe, from time to time. Right now it's a bitch.
But it does not excuse my negligence in not writing. 'I'm sorry.'
The tape radio, would be a dream, and I would love the callander, please.
All sorts of things have been happening here.
Our Christmas mail was stolen for several weeks. The police were called in. A certain screw had convenyently gone sick.
We were given a massive spin. Screws come in from other nicks, unannounced. Within an hour every cell is metal detected, dogged (sniffer). We are all striped naked get an anul probe, just this wing.
The next week over a hundred cons were gone from this wing, to all points. A lot of weapons were found. 'Thank God.' It got a big write up in the local rag.
Other than that life is still, hum drum. There's an awful lot of blacks coming on this wing. That's making the white boys nervous. I remember it was black on white at Long Lartin.
It only takes one punch up between a black or white to start things of god give us strength.
You have my sympathy, with the financial situation out there.

I listen to radio four a lot, and world service. I know things are very bad.

We are lucky in the sence that all our needs are catered for, except sex, unless you like male hoars.

You can never ask me too many questions. Keep them coming.

'What were they?' I will tell all.

You haven't got something to report?

You just sent your last chapter to the publisher. 'GEE WIZZ!'

I wish I could say that. I'v a feeling you are one of life's great understaters.

Could you tell me what ‿‿‿ ‿‿ ‿‿‿ means. It a copy of your hand writing. Even my pakistani mate could read it backwards.

Ask me a question.

See you later

T Shannon
TOM

P.S. Another P.S. for the P.S. army

c/o Prison Reform Trust
59 Caledonian Road
N1 9BU

23rd February 1993

Dear Tom,

What a relief to hear from you again, but my worst fears were correct. That is a terrible scar – they nearly cut you in half! It must have caused you a dreadful amount of pain. And have they cured it, whatever it was? Are you getting better?

I suppose it is an end to swimming and working out in the gym for the time being. That's a worry too. Prison sounds a dangerous place to be unfit in.

In the meanwhile, my mind is racing round all the possible illnesses that it might have been – not that I know much about such things. What was it? Was it colitis?

I had – well have – a friend who was a professor in a university until I persuaded him to leave his cloistered life and enter the cut-throat world of industry. At the last moment there was a hitch. Our company doctor discovered that he had had colitis, which is a dangerous inflamation of the intestine, brought on by stress. The professor wanted to join us nonetheless, and he was such an able guy that we decided to take the chance.

Alas, after a few years, the colitis returned and he had to endure an awful series of operations cutting away his tummy until virtually all that remained was a hot water bottle strapped to his side. I felt so guilty but he had no regrets. 'People who think there is stress in business should try an academic life,' he said, 'That's far worse.' I could imagine that stress in prison is something else again. But I do hope it isn't colitis that you have had.

That search they did and the transfer of half the wing is big drama too. They must have found plenty if they ghosted so many. I hope none were special friends of yours. Things seem to have been more peaceful in the other wings. I enclose a cutting about a Shakespeare play put on in one of the other wings at Maidstone, with a mixed cast of cons and professionals. Did you see it or were you still in hospital?

Yes, I think the country is going through a pretty tough period, especially the unemployed. It is bizarre. All through history, men have striven to get more benefit for less work but now we don't seem able to handle the consequences. Actually, I suspect that we British have got it about right. We don't want to work very hard or become very rich but those bloody Japs and Germans make us feel failures. In the meanwhile, I'm happy to be in about the only growth industry left in Britain – the pensioners. Still, I'm not entirely idle. Here's a little brochure the publishers have issued about my book.

In the meanwhile, I'm sorry about my handwriting. Ann is constantly on about it. She says it shows how senile I am becoming. I'll type them if you like though it always seems a bit cold to me. Better not to be able to read it, in my opinion. You might even think I've said something much more interesting than I really have.

You know that letter you wrote about gangsters. I wondered how they were able to maintain such powerful positions. Bullying? Money? Drugs? Influence outside? Influence with the screws?

I will post your calendar and radio tomorrow. Let me know if they don't arrive.

Yours ever,
Chris

PS I'm afraid I can't find that cutting about the Shakespeare play. Sorry!

Dear Chriss

I hope I find you in good health. The reason you cant find the cutting of the shakespear play is, you have already sent it to me.

I'm like a cat on hot bricks, waiting for the radio and callander. Rush it, rush it, rush it. What a big surprise, reading about your book*. I was expecting a book about your life, army, industry, and country pursuits. Opera! How do you give a surprise whistle on paper?

I'v been sidling up to people and casually telling them that my mate has written a book about the history of Opera.

That was O.K. till someone asked, how come he's writing to a idiot like you?

Our hand writing gets crazy, because we think faster than we can write. Our hand trys to go at the speed we are thinking.

I dont think typing is impersonal. It's the words that matter, or the sentiment, 'Me, slow thinker',

I wouldent call working a farm retirement.

I used to sit and shake with fatigue, after some days working at various jobs on the farms I worked.

I would get £3 a week on the sheep farm at Balquider, Pearthshire. One day off a mounth. Topping and tailing neeps was the worst job. The cold would split the skin on your hands. Tattie howking was the best. Lots of young girls would come from Dundee, Dundee girls – 'AH!' Lambing was a sleep walking job, but very satisfying. My l's look like t's so I keep crossing them.

---

*It is a book called *Don Carlos and Company*. It tells the stories of the real people, like Carlos, who have become heroes and heroines of the opera.

It is no comfort having doc next door, at least not in the medical sence. He's so drug addled he's a useless article. I spend a lot of time on the hustle for him. I wont hustle for drugs for him but tea leaves, sugar, milk, or any goods he needs. Doc is a mounth younger than me, but older in physical or mental stuff, a wreck. But I like the old sod.

I always seem to find someone to look after in every prison I'v been in. I had a 24 year old in Wormwood Scrubs, blond, blue eyed, looking about 19–18. You could see his fear, and aprehension. He was in a recess one time. A jock bully had him by the nuts, and was slapping his face.

I picked up a mop bucket and brought it down on the jocks head. The kid hung around with me like a limpet mine after that. By the time I left the scrubs he had a mate of his own age. Three years later I met him at Long Lartin. He was H.I.V. positive. If there is a god, I'd love to spit in his eye.

There a lot of aids in prison, but mostly from sharing hypos, (needles, known as the works). So if a con approaches one, and says do you know where I can get the works, or, who has the works, he is asking who has a hypo, which means he has some powder to inject, or knows someone who needs a hypo and if he can find a hypo he can make a deal.

You understand? Yes or no, it all comes under the heading, 'hustling'.

There is a man just come in 81 years old, doing a life, killed his misses 79 years old. Normally an old man like that would be treated with respect, and would want for nothing, but, his mouth is like a cesspit, pouring out pure filth. e.g. He asked me for a roll up. 'Certainly Pop,' I said pulling out my snout. 'Don't call me pop, you fucking cunt.' He's a lonely old boy, ah well.

I now earn £8 per week.

I buy 2 oz hiltons dark blend	£3-47
5 packs of fag papers	40
1 large box of matches	<u>50</u>
	4-37

I save the £3-63

Someone asks me, do I want a canteen deal? Yes. So I buy him £6 of goods. He gives me a £10 note for the goods.

His £10 is illegal. He can't buy anything in the canteen with it. He needs the goods, so I have him over a barrel.

I now have a £10 note.

I buy ¹⁄₁₆th of canabis.

Cut it into 6 pieces each worth half an ounce of old holborn = 3 oz

I sell two oz for a ten pound note

I could keep this going for ever, but its not worth the hustle, and would get me in trouble with the barons, who corner the market.

HUSTLING

I buy four Phone cards for £8. Sell them for a £10 note. Again for ever.

All £10 notes eventuly end up with the barons who hands them out on a visit, or to his held screw. A held screw is a screw who is bent (crook), or is blackmailed or just greedy. Or the baron takes the notes out in a charger = usualy a hollow object that goes up your arse.

Let's say someone owes me £50. I pull him up. 'Don't worry,' he says, 'I'v got a home leave soon. I'll come back with an arse full.' He means his arse will have a charger full of herion. Let's say five ounces; that's 141.75 grames cut

81

with shit – talk, baking powder, ground chalk. If only cut in half, you double your volume.

141.75 grammes of herion + 141.75 grammes of shit = 283.50 grammes. It is never cut 50–50. I would say 40 per herion, 60 per shit. Each bag sold is one grame, at £10? That's £3000. On the street herion per ounce is £70 (it moves about). For a layout of £350, pay off = £3000 or more. Run it through your computer. I droped the .50 which would be rounded up to a gram. I hope this makes sence. I wrote it, and Im flummoxed. The mind boggles.

As for male sex, I have never witnessed it. It's just something that goes on. You know who's at it, but stay clear of the type who indulge. I find that stuff more abhorent that drug abuse. I count death by O.D. more worthy than death by aids, homosexual aids.

I will die with a heart attack, or cancer, or old age, barring accidents.

I always say if I ever get out, I will buy a young plump hoor. Perhaps that will be my clog popper. I hope I can manage a drop of Scottish wine as well. Then the devil can have me.

Good luck with the book. It's exciting.

T Shannon
TOM

P.S. No cutting in letter?
P.P.S. Does Ann have a recipe for Coconut Ice, small amount.

6-3-93

Dear Chriss

Thank you, I'm overwhelmed. The tapes are it. Magic. I don't know what else to say. It's just great.

I'v upped my exercise, for the build up to summer routine. One and a half hours, instead of just one during the winter.

I do two hours in the summer, for your joints are more supple in the hot weather. Four afternoons per week.

I do a cell routine of something like TI CHEE. It's something like that routine we did during national service, with the P.T.I. as a mirror, only TI CHEE is in very slow motion.

Doc, is my instructor in TICHEE, so god knows if it even comes close. Never the less, I like to do it.

One of the lads has lent me a skipping roap so I'm into that.

Smooking is a real sod, and it stops me every five minutes, too breathless to go on but I get there.

We have a sports yard. When these old prisons were built, there was no notion of privlages for cons.

So we have a seven a side all weather pitch,

There is a tar walk round the pitch.

The wing 'Med' is built, east to west, long, and north to south, wide.

I live on the north side, west end.

The prison wall runs along the south wall then turns north at the west end.

When I look out my window, and I have to climb on a table to do so, I look straight through the goals, looking north. So the north goal is at the north end of the pitch, away from me.

I'm doing all this in my mind.

So no cheating, and writing it down. Build it in your mind,

or should I say lay it out in your mind. Then draw it one time, and send it to me, line drawing.

Now for the rest of it.

To the east side of the pitch is a tennis court, to the east of that the fence.

To the west side of the pitch is the wall. Arround the pitch is the tar walk.

Across the north end of the pitch is the ediface that holds the (badminton hall, come net ball, and the cirquet gym, and the Multi Gym,) light gym.

Behind that ediface is another same size that holds the swimming pool.

North of the tennis court is a path from the pitch, to the fence.

North of the path is the building that holds the workshops, sewing, and light assembly, the west end of which abuts the tar walk that is on the east side of the pitch.

The south end of the heavy gym is abutted to the west end of the sewing and light assembly, and runs to the north end of the light gym.

Behind the swimming pool, is the workshops, Printers, Book-binders. Running west to east behind the Printers-Bookbinders is the wall running west to east, the west end of the wall meet-ing the north end of the wall running south to north, from the south wall.

Feed that lot into your computer, only if you need to. I don't have a computer.

Soldiers in the days you were in did not have computers. 'But, if you need one?'

I would say there are a horse cart and a half paths between all buildings, and between the wall and everything else.

While you are working on that, 'whats this'?

A wee, wee, man with a red, red coat,
a staff in his hand, a stone in his throat,[1]

---

[1]The answer is a cherry. (I had to ask him.)

I'v enclosed a rixla wrapper. You should buy a pak of rixla and transfer them to this pak. Then get some tobacco, and leave them on the pub table. See what comments you harvest.[2]

Let's hope the Police are not looking for a reprobate when you flash them!!

I seen a cartoon, so I'm going to describe it. There is no one else to talk to behind this door, so you are it!

A van with a load of pop roadies, is traveling down the M.1. A body like a mummy, is being ejected from the back of the van. Did you get it???

Where do they bury sailors?

So where would you bury a roadie?

If you want to tell a joke, and be very dirty about it, cover yourself with soot,!

I got one more joke, so Ill just knock off these two lines, and, start on a clean page.

Well, there's many ways to get rid of two unwanted lines

Now, a lorry delivers bricks to a house.

The resident counts the bricks, one thousand and one.

The occupier tells the lorry driver to take the odd brick back.

The driver throws it in the back of the lorry. The brick is bouncing and banging.

So the driver stops on a bridge, and tosses the brick onto a railway line.

'Funny yes'?

The Callender is nice.

Now, if you will excuss me,

I have three beautiful tapes to listen to.

goodnight

THANK YOU
T Shannon
TOM

P.S. Its just a P.S.

[2]The packet of Risla cigarette papers was prominently marked FOR USE IN HM PRISONS.

c/o Prison Reform Trust
59 Caledonian Road
N1 9BU

25th March 1993

Dear Tom,

I'm sorry that it is so long since I wrote. I've had two from you in the meanwhile. I've been snowed under by my publisher who wanted lots of corrections made and fast. I don't think I've done anything else for about ten days – certainly not any letters, anyway.

I'm glad the Sony works ok. If I was in gaol, I think music would be essential for my staying sane (if I did.). It must be even more so for you. You must have a good voice. I wish I did. I'll try to send you a new tape from time to time. Let me know if you've any preferences.

I enclose my plan based on your description of the gaol. How have I done? I must try to work out a puzzle for you.

Neither of your letters says how you are. Are you getting any better? Has the operation worked? It must have been a big one to leave a scar like that.

We've been digging ponds. We've got an excavator parked on our farm by a contractor who lets us use it. At present the ponds are empty because it refuses to rain. I hope the sides are not drying out. Our clay cracks all too easily in dry weather and the ponds could spring a leak. I'll keep you posted about progress and send you some pictures.

Yours ever,
Chris

Dear Chriss

I don't know when your birthday is. So I thought, I would send you a happy whatever card.

I think it's a good Idea. When you get into birthdays, anniversaries, festifels religious, mothers day, and dads, your talking big money.

So why not a happy whatever card, and small tasty, happy whatever gifts. It means I'm thinking about you.

It could mean. I'm not rich enough to endulge for all occasions, but still remember you from time, to time. It could mean a lot of soft stuff.

Pound to a penny, it would fail. We would still want to communicate on all special occasions. For some reason we all need contact but hate that dependance.

We are the supream lovers, the supream warriers, the power to do anything in our hands.

If ever the human race gets it together, WOW!

We will conquer the Universe.

We will forever search for love.

Death, both natural, and perverse, will come too. We will live forever.

If we don't get it together?

T Shannon
TOM

JOKE

This man walked down the railway platform when he spotted a very young blond, sitting alone, with a little poodle on her lap. So the man went in and sat opposite. The girl, gave him all the come heither stuff.

So he leaned over, and put his hand on her knee, heading for forestry commission property!! The poodle shot forward and said – yip, yip, crr yip yip, crrr yip yip.

So the man tried again, after a sutible rethink.

Same reply from poodle.

I say, said the man, if the **** dog does that again, it goes out of the window. It did, and it did.

ITS A LONG JOKE

At three o'clock the following morning the young blond woke up her husband and said;

'There's someone at the door, sweety.'

'O.K.', says he, and goes to investigate.

There stands the poor, bleeding, bedraggled poodle. And you know what it had in its mouth?

'Go on guess,'

Answer next letter, although you already have it!!

T Shannon
TOM

P.S. NOT BAD, on the layout of this place. I think Ann would be safe in sending you to the post office,
P.S. Cant find card, SORRY.

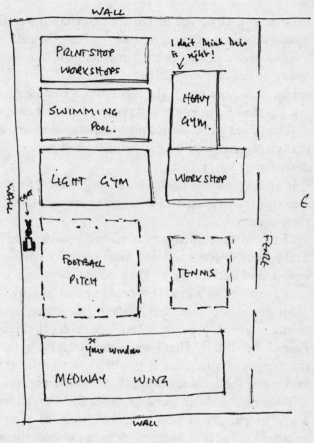

2-4-93

Dear Chriss,

I'll give you eight out of ten for your lay out. I think Ann would be safe in sending you to the Post Office!!

That magic opera, is truly magic.* I'd like to see a real opera. It must be something.

Life here goes on in the same brain nullifying, bourdom (?). The new faces come and go at a hell of a rate.

When I read, and hear, things like that nounce, who killed the father and daughter the shame of being a convicted murderer hangs heavy.

If you sit in the background, and listen to the conversations of the youngsters here, you here them braggin about there crimes.

Listen to this;- One guy is telling how he and his mates broke into a corner shop. Tied the old couple together, naked, and back to back. Then pulled them out of the shop, on a roap tied to a car. This caused great hilarity.

Most of these youngsters have just come up from the young persons prisons. There hard, cruel, and drugged. Pinned they call it. That's when the black bit in the centre of the eyes is smaller than a pin-head, a weird sight. It's like looking at the zombies, from those modern horror movies.

You here a sudden, burst of noise, and shouts, followed by a cry of pain, you pop your head out of your cell, and another knifing is in progress. It happens over the most mundane reasons, a mars bar owed, a half ounce. There's always drugs involved.

The sick parade is longer than the Themes river. There must be some liberal asshole of a doctor, in the surgery. There's a

*Refers to a tape of opera highlights which I had sent him.

thriving trade in pills of all kinds – street legals is the slang name for them. All drugs come under the name 'Gear'. 'Do you know who's holding?', is the constant question.

I'm heart sick, and tired of prison life. This wing is a three ring circus, of self gratification, and evil.

And yet those of us who dont endulge find, and associate with each other.

If I'm not playing cards, I'm playing pool, or matching. I'll send you a piece of my match work soon, almost done it. Just got to varnish it. Did I send you an empty rixla pak?

There will be an empty large box of matches, in the piece of match work. You have to hold the sides of the match box, through the sides, and push the box as normal to present the matches inside. 'No matches coming' – just box.

With the ship on top, you run your thumb nail, along the plimsole line. You will find a raised bit. Keep your nail going. You will unlock the ship.

Open the ship by taking the hull in your nails. You'll see, I hope, 'Keep these instructions'.

The walkman is really something.

We, talk about our penfriends. A few of us who have, know each other, through the system over the years.

I'v got the upper hand over a toffee nosed git, because my penfriend writes about opera. His is nothing but a genteel lady, who has never done anything, but be genteel. He really fancies me. He keeps makeing me cakes.

If he was a sweet looking kid, I might be tempted after all this time. He's the ugliest bastard in the nick. Rotten mutton that thinks its fresh lamb.

He calls me handsome, and throws me secret kisses. It's a fine balance trying to hang on to the cakes. I also use his snooker cue, from time to time. 'It's a tough life'.

Coconut ice is what I'm thinking about. It's pink and white, and hard. I had dreams about it but there gone now. So you don't need to worry. I get eight pounds now, and had some choco-late digestives!! – and a jar of coffee. Living high on the hog.

I'm an instructor for anyone who wants to learn the two machines, I run. If they are drug addicts, I don't entertain them. I got two youngsters from London and Deven and a third from Pakastan. There O.K.

The doc has been told he will be moveing soon. I'll miss the old fellow.

Who, or what moves in next door is in the lap of the gods. 'May the lord have mercy.'

I'm still swimming, pumping iron, still pissing blood. I get severe pains in my chest and abdomen, and I love it.

Pain is a gain. All in the mind. You fight it. I must be doing something right. Word got out that I broke my flask. Now I got two.

I gave my sony to an old tatter called George. He's delighted. Only two cons have seen the walkman tape thing. I have to hide it every time I leave the cell. So the less people that know about it the better,

The toffee nosed git is (was) talking about making chocolate eclairs, so I let him win a few games of pool.

You will not make a lot of money out of your book. There is a lot of opera fans but not enough to make you rich, not like the pop trade.

I keep waiting to here you on classic F.M. or radio four, being interviewed.

You say, you don't want to see the book again. Y'll be bored in a few weeks. Then you'll be into something else.

I got in the half ounce sweepstake for the national. I could use the snout.

Take it easy, soilder, ex tobacco, farmer, and Author, world traveler, Father, and Grandfather. What next?

Well Im off to dream about these eclairs.

Goodnight, till again,

T Shannon
TOM

c/o Prison Reform Trust
59 Caledonian Road
N1 9BU

3rd April 1993

Dear Tom,

Thank you for both your letters. I think a happy whatever card could be a brilliant idea. It's not so much the money saved (which would be its undoing) but it would solve the memory problem. I can never remember when other people have their birthdays which is very embarrassing for they sometimes send me cards. I know a bloke who has the same trouble. His solution was to send all his friends birthday cards on his own birthday instead of theirs. However, he seems now to have forgotten about that too.

I can't wait for the match work to arrive. It sounds amazing.

I'm glad that my book has achieved something! I agree with you – it won't make much money – but chocolate éclairs! He must be a bit of a creep, I think. I guess he feels a bit safer near to you. I think I might look for a friend who knew how to punch if I was in gaol. I used to box when I was young but could never master how to punch really crisply. Mine were always 'push punches'. I'd better learn how to make éclairs while there's still time. Pity he's so ugly – or maybe not. At least you can't catch AIDS from eating éclairs. In the meanwhile, I'm sorry the doc is leaving. From your descriptions of what goes on, it could be as well to have a doc next door.

I haven't got the answer to the riddle. Maybe the dog had the girl's knickers.

In the meanwhile, we've had some rain and got the pond three parts full of water. We had a real downpour and were able to divert part of it through that pipe you see in the enclosed photo. The pond seems to hold water pretty well. It's still pretty raw of course but we'll sow grass and plant shrubs. We hope the wild duck will eventually adopt it and nest on the isle. I am wondering whether to stock it with fish. What would you do?

I also enclose a picture of some of our cattle in the covered yard, lined up on the trough waiting for it to be filled. Just in case you get into any bets, they are, starting with the white-faced one on the left:- Simenthal, Limousin, Charolais, New Zealand grey, Friesian, Limousin, Charolais, Charolais. It looks like another Charolais peeking over the top of the others. Hope you win some money – or at least a mars bar.

The cattle are right to be looking a bit anxious. We're running low on food for them and if this rain continues, we could be in trouble. We don't want to turn them out with the ground like porridge. They would ruin it for the rest of the summer. But we *certainly* don't want to buy in food for them. I am bitterly regretting selling most of our hay when it looked like being a short winter. Still, it seemed a good idea at the time.

We are now busy working out how to grow subsidies rather than crops.

Yours ever,
Chris

8-4-93

Dear Chriss

That pond looks O.K. I like the way you left the tree in the middle. When the pond settles down you can go for a swim. That would keep you supple. It does me. I swim three time a week for twenty mins. If the tree in the pond had been a palm tree, you could swim round it, and look up, and say, I can see your nuts mate!!

I just had the results of my L.R.C.:- LOCAL REVIEW COMMITTEE, My next L.R.C. is to be September 1994. ZUT ALORS.

I'v done your bit of match work. I'm waiting for my favourite screw censor to come back from leave on Sunday 11-4-93. He said he will take care of it for me. He's a good man.

I lost my toffee nosed friend, cakes and all. 'Me and my big mouth.' I introduced him to a huge German fellow whom I knew in the Scrubs. He, le bosch, is now eating my eclairs.

The noise here is terrific. Young blacks trying to outdo each other with there getto boxes, all druged up.

You see the youngsters come from the cantcen with bags stuffed with goodies, just to hand them over to the drug barons. 'It's a shame.'

I'v done the ship before, on matched tobacco tins, but the match box holder is a one off. You can't get tobacco tins now. All is plastic.

I am now writing to a handicap woman at The Lennord Cheshire home, Mote Park, Maidstone. She has been in a wheel chair for yonks. Some muscle waisting decease. Her

95

name is Pat Howes. She asked to come and see me. So I sent her a V.O. telling her that my crime and time had taken there toll on my face. I saw the horror in her eyes when she saw me. I think she had build a picture of a hardened criminal, who dident give a damn. I look like the end results of dorian gray.

To do a murder really eats at the soul. You can be eating a meal, then suddenly think of the person you killed. The food turns to shit, in your mouth.

The doc's still here. He has turned down a prison with open conditions. From there it's a hostel, then freedom.

I think afterr twenty five years he's scared of the outside.

I wish it was me. My first priority would be new fishing gear. Fishing for pike, in the winter is my favourite.

I'v got a picture of a Clydesdale for April, on your calander, a lovely beast.

There's no work till Tuesday, the 13th so I'll have a nap for now, ready for gym this after.

Yours till next
T Shannon
TOM

P.S. Ill send a picture of me. 'Takes time' – awful lot of bull-crap to arrange it
I'm to sing a solo, Easter Sunday. 'This proves I'v got bottle'
P.P.S. The poodle had that brick in its mouth, The one the lorry driver throw over the hump back bridge. 1,001 bricks?

c/o Prison Reform Trust
59 Caledonian Road
N1 9BU

12th April 1993

Dear Tom,

Thanks for your letter. The pond may look inviting but it's going to take a lot to get me in it – in fact, probably an accident! I'm all for keeping fit, but not at that price. Actually, I suppose there will be moments when it would be nice to plunge in. The trouble with farm work is that when you're busy, you're very busy. Often at about 5 o'clock on a hot hay-making day, I've felt how nice it would be to have a swim but, of course, there is time still to bring in four or five more trailer loads. By the time we stop, I'm knackered and hungry and the night air is beginning to congeal the day's sweat. The moment has passed. It's time for a bath not a bathe. Actually, what usually happens is that all those involved sit down, drink beer and get cold and stiff for an hour or so.

I think you're well out of that bloke who was hanging around you. He didn't sound worth the éclairs. I am very interested to hear about Pat Howes. You must be careful. You probably mean a lot to her. It must be terrible to have one of those wasting diseases. I bet she looks daily for your letter, even now when she knows what you look like. If we ever meet, I hope I won't wince. I don't think I will. I look at a picture of Dorian Gray every morning in the mirror.

For some twenty years I had a beard. I grew it for a joke, really, but then could not take it off without – well, losing face. However, after I retired, it began to irritate me. I thought I looked such a stupid old goat. So one day on holiday with Ann, I shaved it off. I was appalled by what had been happening underneath it. It really was a Dorian Gray effect. I went out and saw Ann wince – just like Pat Howes. Ah, well. One just has to get used to it.

I think you ought to talk to someone about Fred. I am sure it does harm to bottle it up. I believe people often find it easiest to talk about things to a complete stranger but I suppose it's hard to find one in prison. Of course, it's not necessary to kill someone to have memories that knot one's stomach with horror. The Catholics sure knew what they were doing when they invented the confessional. God knows why the Protestants dropped it.

I am stunned to hear that the doc's been in for 25 years. Whatever did he do? It doesn't sound like your LRC went too well. I suppose you did not go to it. You want to watch out or you'll end up like the doc. I'd have thought the racket of all those ghetto blasters would have made you and the doc absolutely determined to get out as soon as possible! But I can see his problem. It's a chill world on your own.

I don't seem to have too much news at the moment. I've been spending too much time hammering away at my book.

Yours ever,
Chris

PS Herewith coconut ice recipe.
PPS I'm too stupid to get the joke about the poodle. A brick!?
PPPS Surely you shouldn't still be pissing blood and having so much pain. You never told me what the illness was but it doesn't sound right – whatever it was.

Medway Wing
HM Prison
County Road, Maidstone
Kent ME14 1OZ

15-4-93

Dear Chriss

Please thank Ann for the recipe for coconut ice. The kitchen area is being renovated right now so it will be some time before, I can try the recipe.

I just got back from the gym so I'm na-card.

The match box is done, so I'll have to wait till the wing censor returns from leave, at the end of this month. He said to bring it to him, and he'd take care of the postage. So I'll wait.

A couple of carp will be just right for your pool, leather carp or crucian, or common carp, and a couple of tench, and a few roach and perch. These are pool fish. The carp were brought to this country by monks as a food fish. They and the tench keep the bottom clean, and stirred up. The four fish I mention are good course fishing fish, Tench are a shole fish, so if you hook one, get back in for another. There match winners.

When bream are young they are a lovely silver colour, and are called skimmers in the midlands. Probaly got outher names around the country,

But carp common, or crucian are the kings.

I once hooked a 37lb carp, What a thrill that was! I got it on a half inch cube of luncheon meat. Ah well, those were, etc, etc.

If you want to cook a trout, put a bit of fennel and a very liquid ½ desert spoon of hot mustard or curry, inside the fish, wrap it in a sheet of news paper, the Times or the Guardian, soak it ringing wet, put it in a hot oven. When the paper is very dry unwrap and the skin will come off with the paper. Lovely stuff. 20 mins. Eat it from the paper. Then, when finished, scrunch paper and dump. No dishes to wash.

My wages now £7 flat, with bonus. 'millionair, soon me.' We can see the sports field from the print shop.

The youngsters watch there mates with envy. So I tell them all the doges for getting off work. They give me a cheery wave from the sports area, and because they are not at work there wages go into a kitty to be shared out at the end of the month. 'What an evil old sod I am,' as the sonic boom said, to humty dumpty. Never give a dum egg an even break.

Young criminals, and some not so young, are very brutal. There is a small number who try to be respectfull to older cons like me. But most of the youngsters, cheet and misuse each other. They rip each other off. All, or most of there quarrels are about the most trivial stuff, like an half ounce owed or a mars bar.

This is what I heard one boy saying on the phone, to his mother.

'I cant wear that cheep shit. There garbage.' he was talking about a pair of shoes, called trainers. He sold them for a sixteenth of gear (canabis). They cost his mum £75, but they were last year's fashion.

Convicts are encouraged to wear ther own clothes. Its cheeper for the governor, as he is now to answer for all prison expenditure. There are only a few cons like me who wear prison clothes, as we don't have families to pounce off.

There is some nice light blue paper in the print store. As soon as I can get my theaving hands on it, I'll be able to write more in one letter, My name on the letter board gives me a buzz. Thank you,

till again,
T Shannon
TOM

Medway Wing
HM Prison
County Road
Maidstone
Kent ME14 1OZ

[undated]

Dear Chriss

I'll tell you a bit about racial stuff in prison.

The majority of whites do not, or will not associate with the blacks, and vice-verca, The asians keep very much to them selves, are very quiet and friendly, but, I think think this is because they believe that being polite, and humble, saves them a lot of trouble. I suppose that's true. Almost every asian is doing time for drug smugling. They have an insatiable greed for money, and education. Those that deal in money, or drugs in prison, have a strong white as there go between. You always feel you are being used by or manipulated by asians.

They will suddenly offer you small kindnesses, for a few days. Then ask you to do something. There kindnesses then stop. I live among the asian community on this wing, and although I'm a loner, I'm a great watcher of people being sucked in by the asians. And sure enough, its not long before they are doing, or delivering something to the asians. But, you never feel any threat from the asians. I have one who hangs about me like a leach. He is a skinny, consumptive little bloke. I now even have him as my second man on the cylinder press. I suppose I'm some sort of protection for him, But I like him, so thats O.K.

Now, for the afro caribeans, some are very good, but the arrogance of the majority is appalling. They really think that the rest of us are shit, and treat us as shit. Most of them are scagheads. There crimes are terrible. If there is a white nounce on the wing, the whites will ignore him, or even attack him, or burn him out. If an afro nounce is on the wing the other afros will tell you;- 'He only rape honky bitch. What honky bitch for man?' (any white person is a honky). But I must admit if an afro is in for child molestation, the other afros will see to him or if he is in for a sex crime against black girls. But as for white girls, thats O.K. 'All white women pant for black man. Once black man have white woman she never want honky again' – so the afros believe. I tell them white women only chase black men to get her handbag back. The politicians can sing as loud as they like about how good race relations are in this country, but down here among the criminals the hatred can be cut with a knife, its so thick. The racial tension among afroes, and whites, is tremendous. But its not so bad here, as it was in Long Lartin. There they had got to the point of cutting each other. Whites are basically a fist fighting people. The afroes are a knife pulling lot, but so far they have only cut each other. The white gangster paracite class, all go to the gym. They are scared. The afros get anything they want by there voices. 'Give me a rollup man. Man, Give Me a rollup. WHAT? MAN GIVE ME A ROLL UP. **WHAT? A DON BELIVE IT. OLD MAN DON LIKE BLACK MAN. <u>GIVE ME ROLL UP MAN</u>**.' They don't ask me anymore. Tenacity, and a fuck off smile always wins. And yet some of the afros are gentlemen. As for the whites, we are everything the asians, and the afros are, and more. The devil has won, or am I living in hell.

till again
T Shannon
TOM

P.S. what is this –   0
                        MA   !!
                        BA
                        PHD

THREE DEGREES BELOW ZERO

Dear Chriss

I heard a fascinating programe on the radio, about the prison system, in the U.S.A. Prison rehabilitation. Was a Swedish Idea way back when.

It has since been found, by the yanks and other countries that rehab dosen't work. I have watched young men, and some not so young, comeing into, or onto these wings. It's like coming home for them.

You see there eyes darting about, Then they spot someone they know, and a shout goes up 'Hay Tony! Hay Billy!' Then Billy runs down the stairs, grabs Tony, like he was a long lost friend. (The youngsters all like to live on the threes, top landing)

Then Billy says;- 'Charlie's here, and Noz and Pep. Moke's on Kent.' You can see Billy relax. 'He's home.' (They all have nick names.)

I often said to doc, I'm sure these kids love comeing into prison. There lives must be miserable outside.

And sure enough, the radio programme says the same. This yank professor says that these youngsters, are in a state of excited anticipation when comeing in, and are in a state of low expectation when going out, although they pretend otherwise.

I honestly think that once we are allowed T.V.s in our cells some of these kids will never be wanting to leave prison. 'It is quite literary there home.' They are totally inadiquit outside. They just don't know how to survive, outside. There crimes are so petty. They are requests to get back inside, back home.

Yet a strange thing happens. Within in a few weeks, they are in a stuper of lathargy. The novelty of comeing home has worn off. They are the prison Zombies, the lost, the lonely, the damned.

I must be like a father figure or something. I get all there stories, there hopes, there dreams, there wishes. All start with, 'when I get out.' I'v got one of them into a beginners reading class. I have to now and again listen very secretly to his progress. His eyes glow with pride, when I praise his efforts. When I leave his cell, I clance back, and he is into his book. He is hungry for more praise. I'll shock my mum, he says. I hope she is intelligent enough to show him her pride in him. Still he will be down this evening, (saturday) to read the page I set for him. My astonishment at his progress, will set him up for the next page. He gave me his apple this week, and I fell about laughing. He's puzzled over this. (Think about it).

I hope you like this box. I saw the ship on a tobacco tin some years ago, and I have been carring it about in my head.

The box is a match and veneer sandwich. You can see the veneer if you look at the side panels. I can't varnish too well.

Run your thumb along the plimsole line. You will unlock the ship. Grip the front of the rear half of the hull, with your thumb and index finger nails, and lift. Close it front half, then back half, then lock again!! Put a new box of matches in.

T Shannon
TOM

P.S. My spleen was punctured.
Don't ask, just a stab

c/o Prison Reform Trust
59 Caledonian Road
N1 9BU

23 April 1993

Dear Tom,

Three letters have arrived from you <u>and</u> the matchbox! I don't know where to start. I think I must start with the matchbox holder.

Tom! It is an absolute miracle! I don't know how to thank you adequately. I can't tell you how much wonder it is arousing – the detail, the mechanism to open the secret compartment, the hinges of the doors, the accuracy of the matchwork, the whole concept and the design. It is a modern equivalent of those ships the prisoners of war made during the Napoleonic War. I can't imagine how long it took you to make. What patience it must have needed – what steadiness of hand. It is already one of our proudest possessions and a big talking point whenever anyone comes to the house. Your ears must be burning all the time! Thank you very, very much. It is beautiful.

Before going on to the letters, I have to say something about that stab wound. I suppose I should be happy because I had quite made up my mind that you had colitis – but a stab wound! You say nothing of how you got it but I suppose it must have been connected with the business of the Stanley knife.* But how awful. What terrifying places gaols are.

---

*I later found out I was wrong. It had been a random stabbing when Tom answered a truculent young thug back in kind. The weapon was a 'shive' [rhyming with give]. This is not prison slang, according to Tom, but the correct word for a home-made knife. My *OED* does not list it but, under the etymology of to shiver into pieces, it mentions it as an obsolete word for slice. What is obsolete for an editor may be all too current for a convict. The shive had punctured Tom's spleen which had had to be removed.

This comes through from everything you say in your letters. I have read them and re-read them and really thought about them. You don't realize that what seems ordinary to you is absolutely extraordinary to an innocent like me. I didn't even know that I was a honky. Most of all, I've been thinking about your third letter where you describe how young cons get to regard gaol as home. Of course, I had heard that before but you describe it so vividly. It is terrible. What is to be done? I can hardly bear to think of that young con slanging his mum for sending last year's trainers.

I am going to take your advice about stocking the pond. I had got myself a book about fish and it agrees with you – as does my neighbour, though what he knows about the subject I would not know. However, I think I'll let it settle down for a year. It needs to build up a strong population of insects and wiggly things. I have scooped a few buckets out of other ponds which teem with life but I think I should give them a year to multiply before they have to cope with hungry fish.

That was one hell of a carp you caught! 37lbs! The biggest river fish I ever caught was 16lbs and I nearly died of excitement with that. There was another time when I was in Aden when we were out early in a little dhow, trying to catch baby barracudas for breakfast (delicious but no good by lunchtime). We used sometimes to catch small sharks too which were a nuisance. They used to thrash about the boat snapping at our legs and it was hair-raising trying to get the hook out of their mouths. One morning, just before dawn, something tightened my line and then started to pull so hard that I had to wind it round a rowlock in order to hold it. Very slowly at first but with gathering speed, the boat began to move and whatever it was started to tow us out to sea. After we'd gone about ten yards, thank God the line snapped. I never saw what it was but I expect it was a big shark. It made us think because it was lying just where we often used to go scuba diving.

Ann's got your recipe for trout. Now I'll have to catch one.

Finally, (because I must stop – it's very late) thanks for the poem by Simon Rae. I liked it very much. I've put it in the secret compartment of the matchbox holder.

Yours ever,
Chris

PS It will be a little while before I write again. I'm off to France to search for illustrations for my book.

Dear Chriss

It had to happen. Prisoners are now muggin prisoners.

I had been talking to a young fellow who has come from a y.p. prison,

I was asking him why y.ps were topping themselves (suicide). This is what he told me (some of it). He arrived at reception of the young offenders place, was left sitting in the holding area for three hours, then was prosessed. The first question he was asked was, 'Name?' Answer;- 'Shannon.' The screw stood and slapped him up the side of his head. 'You call me sir. Name?' Answer;- 'Piss off.' 'Oh dear,' said the screw, and the prosessin carried on, till the lad got to the shower. Then four other lads kicked the shit out of him, till the screw said enough.

The screw lifted his head up by the hair and said;- 'You call me sir.'

The lad then went on about other staff.

Then he said;- 'There's one bastard con I want to meet, in or out.' 'Who's that?' I said. 'The bastard who mugged me for my parcel, him and his mates.' 'Tell me what happened,' I said, and he did.

The lad knew he was going down, so he had a quarter of canabis and £25 in a charger [cigar shaped object] up his bum. When he was settled, he went to the bogs to retreve his charger. He never made it back to the dormatory.

I was telling this to some of the cons I work with.

'Fucking hell Tom, where you been? That stuff goes on in every nick.'

108

'Well,' I said, 'I'v been in seven years. I'v never heard of it. So they whistled up a kid from the bookbinders. Tell pops (thats me) what happened when you come back from home leave.

The kid showed me two cuts, (superficial by now). His parcel was forced out of him by two skag heads. (He's one too, hence the parcel.)

One of those skagheads I have always found polite and easy with me. I asked him if it was true. All he said was, 'I got it bad pops.' So I said;- 'Why don't you see the quack, and tell him you have a habit and get the sub they give out.' 'I ain't got a fucking habit pops'

I'll give you a mark, Christopher, and mark it well. It wont be long before murders are done over hard drugs in prison.

Yet the most simple, and basic tests, would prove who is, and who is not a drug abuser.

Do you wonder, why I keep fit, and, go in hard at the first hint of a threat. '**FEAR**' I'm so scared, and tence in prison. I wish Fred would come back and say its all a big mistake.

I hope you will forgive my language in these letters, I have to tell it as it comes over, or it would not sound right. 'What do you think?' I could put F******. Do you 'read asterisk'?!! Anyway as a x squddie you could teach me a little french. It's 3 in the morning, some sleep later.

T Shannon
TOM

Thanks for the kind words
about the box. You polished my star.

Dear Chriss,

I got pissed at an article in the Daily mail.

It stated we had T.V. – Showers, in our cells, and a lot of other stuff. I have at times stood in a bowl and poured water over myself, when the showers break down.

It too cold to go to an upper landing. There's no showers unit on the twos landing and all the air vents are on the threes landing.

So the higher you go, the colder it gets and besides, I dont want the other cons seeing me out of breath, at the top of the climb. Wait a minute. I'll roll another fag!!

Ther's a kid, I used to do gym with. He was an amature boxer, but turned to picking up queers and cold cocking them, then robbing them. This is called 'rolling queers'.

Anyway, this kid is down here on accumalated Visits. 'Oh God!' Now I'm going to have to explane Accumalated Visits!!

Say, I was in living in Dundee prison, and my family lived in cornwall. It could be I am in Dundee to get what I need in the way of education, or trade, or something.

So to save my family a fortune in fares or gas, I save my visiting rights up and once a year, get 1 mounth, or 1 month now and 1 later. The tax payer gets hammred again, with massive transport bills.

I went from Pentonville to Long Lartin in a single decker bus, the kind of bus that goes abroad, with television at intervals, above the seats, with six escort screws.

I was turned away from Long Lartin. They were in dispute, and not accepting.

Back to london, same coach – Scrubs this time. 1 month later, back to Long Lartin – again alone, another six screws, another luxury coach. 'I tell ya boy, A travel in style', I hope group four moves me next!! 'Anyway where was I?'

I meet this kid in the gym, and he puts me through my paces, 'Why didint I just say that at the start?'

Something really good happened today. I got a bird. I have to say bird, as I dont know how to spell budgerigar. I got the cage, a big bunch of seed, and scratch paper, and bird toys.

He's all yellow with black tracery and he's great. The guy's gone home. He gave me a pair of civie shorts, a tee shirt, 1 jeans, 1 track suit bottoms, all civies. What with other bits given to me, I'm starting to be a dandy. 'I fink it wuff wiles dwessing well.' I hope to god some arshole dosent tell me I look the business.

Still, some of the clothes the kids wear, make them look like a chiness lantern party.

I keep waiting to hear you on the radio, about your book. Maybe on classic F.M. If so, Ill tell the bird. 'I know him, and you know what bird! that picture above your head is all his cows.' Dear, dear, what am I saying. Do give Ann my kindess regards!! Yes, well, Ahem,

So your in France. Eating, patty the fat grass, and eggs car gos. If you come across a young bardot who wants to be a pin up, I got a wall, four of them. I hope you find the right pictures.

A youngster asked, how, he could get a body like mine. A bit deflatory, having to admit that it takes forty five years of neglect.

You should never ask a lived in person a piss taking question, in front of others!!

When I told him his pink little nipples turn me on, the rest of him went the same colour,

'coffee time'

A lot of nigling things are going on here. This evening, raw eggs are being thrown at the screws, from the upper landings. One femail screw got a bucket of water dumped on her from above.

111

I can't see the point of it all. The screws here bend over backwards to be nice.

One screw said, to a lad with his plate full of grub. They feed you pigs well. This was a lad the screw has had a laugh and joke with. You even see them restling with each other, but, the screw was overheard by other cons, who took it seriously. The screw was on the hot plate at dinner time (evening). As every con got a dollop of creamed spuds from him, they gave a loud 'Oink, Oink'

I'm not fed up listening to the tapes. I treat them as treats to be heard from time to time.

I'm in the process of making a box for the tapes. It will hold twelve, when done ('not a hint'). It will be lined with the best book cover stuff, and veneered outside. You will be getting ponced for a catch for the box, when I know what size I want (unless one turns up – I'v got the pounce out).

Not another bleeding page,?

I found that card I was talking about. Sorry I have to fold it. 'Work for you.' You can cut the gremlin out, glue it onto a piece of tarpaulin, or tent material, at least two inches bigger than cut out, pin it to a clean piece of paper, lay it on a flat surface, sellotape the paper to the surface, then give it a nice coat of varnish. After 48 hours another. Do this four times, but always cover the work with the lid of a shoe box to keep off the dust motes. A clean dust free corner of the environment is called for. When all coated and dry, trim material to what you want. Then sew on to whatever. After all it is a happy whatever card. I don't know what washing it will do. 'Clear varnish mind'.

You should get the Boots sounds right catalogue. Some lovely stuff in there to turn your grand kids on to music. (Not cheap).

Did any of your kids take to opera?

Im to go up north soon, I think. I was asked what prison I would like to go to. I told them to pick one. 'A nick, is a nick.' I quite like this one, but I dont know how to show it. I have this stupid KEEP OFF ME facade. When I'm banged up, I'm as free as I can be, in prison. When I'm on the pool table, I'm alive. I love the game. 'PHEW' all done.

T Shannon
TOM

Dear Tom,

I found your two letters when I got home from France. It took me several days to find what I wanted but quite entertaining. I spent one whole day in the archives of the French National Library with a very pretty young French archivist. I behaved my age. Ah, well.

Anyway thank you for both letters. No, I don't read asterisk. Ann and I just say fuck when we feel like it.

I have been feeling like it ever since reading that story of the kid whose parcel was cut out of his bum. I can't bear to think about it but I can't stop thinking about it. What terrible things drugs are that they drive people to such cruelty. I've probably said in one or two of my letters how I believe the only solution is to make drugs not exactly legal but not criminal – ie. a drug user could get his supplies but would have to accept supervision and treatment. Your story of the skaghead, one of the two that cut this boy's bum open, makes me wonder if I'm right. It would not work if drug users refused to admit they were hooked and preferred illegal drugs. I suppose they hate the idea of losing their independence. In the end they lose it anyway – but they may not believe that. Ah well, I'm a great one with my firm opinions about things I don't actually know anything about! You are helping to cure me of this bad habit.

As a tax-payer, I am stunned to hear about how you travel when you are ghosted. How can it be? A luxury coach and six screws each time? I suppose it's one of the screws' perks that was overlooked when they introduced Fresh Start.

I am not too sure what to make of your happy whatever card. He's well done but he's not pretty. Still, he looks as though he might have a sense of humour. I am trying to decide whichever he's most suited for. Certainly not Christmas.

I'm not sure what news I've got for you. Did I tell you that we'd been able to turn the cattle out at last? It is such a pleasure simply to stop feeding them and bedding them down every day. Mind you, it doesn't save any time. We still have to walk round them every day to make sure they are all there and alright. It can be quite nice to do. I suppose most cons would give their eye teeth just to be able to!

These warnings of an impending move must be most unsettling. It must be difficult enough to establish a position in a gaol but when you move, you lose all that and have to start all over again. Still, it sounds as though Maidstone is building up for trouble again. There must have been more to it than that remark by the screw about feeding the pigs well – and I thought the oink-oinks hilarious but raw eggs and buckets of water make me feel sorry for the screws. One can see how they get cynical.

Yours ever,
Chris

FOUR

THE CELL

In replying to this letter, please write on the envelope:

Number . . . C61329 . . . Name . . . SHANNON

MEDWAY WING
HM PRISON
COUNTY ROAD
MAIDSTONE
KENT ME14 1UZ

7–5–93

Dear Chriss

I am on the move to H.M.P. BLUNDESTON
LOWESTOFT
SUFFOLK
NR32 58G

I'm to arrive there on the 11-5-93 Tuesday.

I'v been asking cons who have been there. They all say its a pisshole, full of skagheads.

Well, I'm prepared to give any prison a look over.

I hope, I find you, and yours well. All this traveling must tire you out. The change of diet, you must be used to with the life you have led.

I have to cut this short as I have a lot of rigmarole to suffer, due to the move. My next letter will be from suffolk,

Wish me luck as you wave me goodby, cheerio here I go on my way. 'O LOR NOT AGAIN'

T Shannon
TOM

P.S. (GOT ONE) I'm trying to find an envelope to send you a booklet that will astound you, as to the number of prisons in England – Wales,*

*He sent me a booklet called *Visiting Prisons*. There were 130 prisons listed.

119

c/o Prison Reform Trust
59 Caledonian Road
N1 9BU

10th May 1993

Dear Tom,

Your letter about your move to Blundeston has only just
reached me. I'm afraid this letter will be too late to welcome
you there and to wish you well in your new gaol. I do wish
all these things, of course.

I think you are right not to believe everything bad they say
about Blundeston. It may be a gaol to warm Judge Tumim's
heart! As I said in my last letter, I do sympathize with you
moving at all. It is so hard to build up and establish one's
position in a society. To be made to throw it all away and to
begin again from scratch is a great burden. But if you've
done it once, you can do it again.

Anyway – lots and lots of good luck.

Yours ever,
Chris

Dear Chris,

I arrived here just after five on 11-5-93.

The ride up was fantastic. The sun was shining. The whole world was sparkling.

Saw a strange sight, a field full of little huts, with pigs round the doors, like villagers round there cottage doors. The kid I was handcuffed to asked me what it was. I told him it was a screws maternity ward.

I was put on to A Wing. When I walked into the cell, I nearly fainted. The walls were covered in excrement, toothpaste, and goodness knows whatelse. The next day, I refused to cooperate in any induction processes until they found me a cleaner cell.

There was no 'O.K., hang on till we find you a cleaner cell.' It was 'your nicked,' and off I went to seg, £1 fine.

I have since refused to return to the wing, till I'm found a cell that's fit for human habitation. But they just come into the seg cell and order me back to the filthy cell on A WING. I refuse. Another fine. The total is now £7.

I have gone on hunger strike. I'm <u>STARVING</u>.

My belly sounds like the drum section of the black watch pipe band, but I will keep up my protest till I get a clean cell. In the mean time, I play patience, read, listen to the sony tape radio (batteries gone).

The S.O. in this seg unit has asked me;- 'Animals are fussy where they live these days, aren't they',?

'Well bollox to him.'

I can't tell you much about this place just yet.

The security fencing around this place is massive. It makes me wonder if it was built for cat 'A' prisoners, such as the I.R.A., the crays and the blakes of this world.

I talk to the other inmates by shouting through the cage outside the windows. They all seem to say this place is a piss hole, full of smack heads. (I dont know what smack heads are, yet.) They say that 'A' Wing is solid iron, (iron hoof – poof.) If this is so, the few inmates I saw on A WING must be the ugliest poofs in the world, god help me. I wonder how much a pair of stainless steel under pants will cost me?!! (MUST SLOP OUT)!

(Well, that was a delightful experience)!

There's no toilets and sinks in these cells. We have to use gissunders. I did not bring the bird. A young indian had him, cage and all. I may get one or two, when I'm out. I liked him.

I forgot to pack my writing paper, so I'm down to useing this old jotter. I used my reception letter to write to Angela Rumbold, the minister for prisons. There's another brick wall for my head,

Well, perhaps these people will find me a clean cell, and I can get on with my sentence. If not,?

There's a blackbird singing outside the window. I hope he is a regular visitor.

There are 160 bricks in the wall at the foot of my bed. I'v counted them over and over, again and again.

I wonder if I missed one?

Yours
T Shannon
TOM

c/o Prison Reform Trust
59 Caledonian Road
N1 9BU

19th May 1993

Dear Tom,

God, how awful! I hope you don't mind but I at once con-
tacted the Prison Reform Trust for advice. They offered to
write to the Governor but I asked them not to, at least till I
had heard your views.

They also offered two bits of advice:-

[a] stop your hunger strike. They say that hunger strikes
<u>never</u> work in prison.

[b] ask to see a member of the Board of Visitors. These are
apparently not your ordinary prison visitor full of foggy
good will. The board is charged with the responsibility of
protecting prisoners rights. You have the right to see one, or
indeed, all of them. Of course, you would have to convince
them of your complaint.

I think it is scandalous, what is happening to you and I've
tried to imagine why it is happening. Give a dog a bad name,
the proverb says. I suppose you do have one!

Reading your letter, I was reminded of the experiences of
a man with an unpronounceable Greek name who writes in
Ann's comic (the Spectator) under the name of Taki. A year
or so ago, he was caught with an envelope of drugs in his hip
pocket and sentenced to 18 months. Being a toff and small,
he expected all sorts of trouble and got it. The first was a
shitty cell like yours. His reaction was to ask for scrubbing
brushes and disinfectants and, ignoring the smirks of the
screws, he had it spotlessly clean within a day. He felt he had
won because he had refused to be provoked by them.

Being small and very rich, he had trouble in association

too but, like you, he knew how to handle himself. He is an amateur boxing champion and a judo black belt. He had his fights with the bullies, after which he was left alone. He fought when the fight was fair but when it was loaded against him, by the screws, he adopted a different plan.

Your letters are quite as interesting as his articles (though your style is a bit different). It makes me wonder whether they should not be published. I think people would be very interested in what you have to say.

I won't bother you with any of our affairs in this letter.

Yours ever,
Chris

In replying to this letter, please write on the envelope:

Number ... C61329 ... Name ... SHANNON ...

HOSPITAL UNIT
NORWICH PRISON
NORWICH

Dear Chriss

Don't even think of answering these letters, until I have settled somewhere.

I got my tapes, thank you.

I have no batts, but my lady probation officer in Birmingham, has sent me £10 out of the blue, so I will have no problem getting batts, when I settle down.

I carried on with my hunger strike at Blundeston. Eight screws came into my cell and bundled me off to this place.

Boy oh Boy, was I scared! I was expecting the liquid cosh.

I thought I would not be able to write to you again, as the L. cosh tends to cabbage one. I'v seen its results on others.

So far, so good. But the nearvousness of what might happen next is still with me.

This unit is clean, and well run, and very peacefull. So if they dont play head games with me, the rest, away from the tensions of ordinary location will do me good. I wish I could take this bed here with me. I'v had the best nights sleep, for a long time. All I had in the seg was a blanket. What happens next? Where to next?

My mind is still in turmoil over what is happening to me. So I will write more, when Im settled down.

I am gasping for a smoke.

Thank you for the tapes. They look interesting. 'Aint life a ball!!'

Zut alors
T Shannon
TOM

125

21-5-93

Dear Chriss

I think, and I hope everything is back to normal.

I'm back on normal location, A Wing again. My god, I find hard to believe that it took such pain just to have a clean cell.

There are cleaning officers on every wing, of every prison, who's job it is to see that cells are in a clean state for incoming inmates.

It's not as if they have to pick up a brush or mop themselfs. They have a team of cleaners for that purpose.

I wrote to Angela Rumbold, twice, in very strong words.

The chief medical officer at Norwich, Dr Khan, came to the hospital cell, and had a twenty minute talk with me. He went apeshit when I explained the circumstances.

'Leave it to me,' he said, 'I'll sort that lot and there canteen mentality out, through the Home Office.'

He then shook hands with me, and hay presto I'm back in a clean cell.

I begged and begged for someone to go and look, just look at the cell. All I got was – you will return to that cell, or go on ajudication.

Seven times, seven pounds fines.

I even had a visit from a governor who came to explain the importance of maintaining discipline in prison. I told him he was a weak kneed whimp, and the P.O.A. bullies had him, and his prison, by the short and curlies because of the time it took to sort it out.

I found out the lad who had that cell made that mess, with his own excement, as some sort of protest against the system.

Idiots like him. dont stop to think, that it is some other con who has to live with the results.

The works screws are in the process of painting these cells. One of them said it would take them a week to scrape that one cell. 'AH WELL' IT'S OVER

This paper, and envelope stamped, are just the job. I hope your not out of pocket. I could afford paper and stuff if I gave up smoking.

When I have no tobacco, I leap out of bed in the wee hours, looking for something to kick.

I hardly sleept a wink last night, so I went through a bit of snout.

This pen writes in lumps.

I left the bird with a young asian, who coveted it. I don't think I should have another just yet. Just in case of repercussions. The powers that be are crafty. They may find some way of getting back at me. Still it does make the time fly.

I loved those patches of yellow rape seed on the way here. I see some of it in the verges. Will it take over like the dandelion? The yanks, when I was there, were fighting a looseing battle with the dandelion.

I'm in the stage right now where no one talks to you. They don't know who I am, or what. One of the wing bullies has been eying me, I eyed him right back. He was two sinks away from me when we got out to wash. I said to the youngster between us. Who's the wing bully son. The kid gave a side look, and the same to the bully, then lowered his head further into the sink. I bent down to the kids ear, and said I suppose I'd reconnise them in the shower. They always have tiny pricks, and hardly any balls. I caught the bully's eye in the mirror, winked and muted a kiss. He left the washroom. Best to get it over with, 'What do you think,'? Otherwise, this eyeballing can go on for ever.

I am sorry to lay that stuff on you. It is hard on your own, you think. They could do anything to you, and no one would be any the wiser. Writing to you has become a release valve.

I don't know about writing a book. If you haven't kicked the bucket by the time I'm released, (you wouldent do that to me, I hope), you could just publish the letters as they come to you. Don't correct them in any way. You could call the book 'Letters from over the wall,' or, 'The meanderings of a muppet,' or 'See what I let my self in for'.

Here's a bit of graffety I saw on the cell wall at Norwich hospital. 'All I want is food, shags, fags, and a kip,' Till again

T Shannon
TOM

Sunday 23 may

Dear Chriss,

All that noncence the last few days has left me shattered.

I can hardly get myself off this bed.

But, first let me thank you for the parcel that arrived this morning.

To see all the expectant cons, hanging around the letter board, waiting to see if there names go up, and it is a real thrill when yours does. When you open up the package, and see all the stuff. You swallow the lump for a second or too. 'Thank you so much'.

You see kids reading there letters, walking into things or other cons, such is there eagerness to hear from someone.

Its like, someone knows me. I dont know but you must know what I mean. You must have seen the kids in the army getting letters from home. There deaf, dumb, and blind to everything or anyone, till the thing is read (<- not right is it)

Then you see them rushing off to tell there mates, what's in the letters.

You see some young cons go to the letter board everyday, and there faces drop. I like to reach out to some of there famileys and shake them by the neck.

I think just one letter a week would save some of these cons from seeking comfort and sucker, somewhere else. 'There I go again.'

I just been locked up, seven minutes to eight. Enough for this day – 'more tomorrow.' 'Good Night.'

I'll listen to my new tapes now.

2AM 23-5-93

Wolfgang Amadeus Mozart – it says on the blurb, Gera Anda, Piano and conductor. How can you play and conduct at the some time?

There's a picture of a lovely girl on the blurb. Is that Gera Anda? If it is she must have some bottle.

I heard Mozart before. I used to live with a voice teacher. She used to wax lyricle about Mozart, and teach me how to speak English 'like what it should be spoke'!! mate. I'll save Shubert for another time. 'We dont want overkill, do we'?

That Ludwig Van Beethoven – I had the volume on loud the first time I played it. It caught me by surprise. I nearly hit the roof with that start.

There's a big lake just the other side of the fence. We get a lot of ducks come into the prison grounds. Some strange looking ducks. The cons just walk round them. The ducks dont pay the slitest attention to the cons. I get the feeling the con who tried to horn them, would get a black eye. There's lots of pied wagtails, like little victorian ladies shaking there bustles up and down. I got a bit of sunburn today.

I got to tell you about Fred soon. It's boiling my brain, having him in there. It's crippling me. I just can't talk to prison staff. 'Shit heads.'

T Shannon
TOM

Its a wee square world, is my world,
Its bounderies very close,
It is my womb, my haven,
Just right, for a liveing goast,
a door, bang, bang, bang's.
a rageing cry is heard,
someone didint get his fix
dispare,
only the junky care's,
Im alright,
I got mine
hay man, Im doing fine,
I dont care,
I dont give a dam,
In my wee square world
I know, who I am.

There's a little bird,
with me tonight
a lovely thing
a pretty sight
they say she came,
from a land thats, far,
I like my little,
Budgerigar,

You have heard the saying, he's as thick as two short
planks.

We had a fellow in maidstone, who was known as the vil-
lage Idiot, or shortplanks,

Shortplanks was sitting on a wall with some fellows, when
he says – aint some pigeons really fat.

Its all the bread we throw out the windows for them, says
one of the cons.

There the best kind – says another. Best for what? – says
planks.

Eating – says the con – the yeast in the bread makes the meat tender. If you can catch one, planks, pluck it, and stuff it with minced up sausages, onions, and brown bread. It melts in your mouth when cooked.

You could see short planks looking at the birds with a new intensity. The next day his windowsill was covered with bread.

After a few weeks of trying, planks caught a big fat pigeon. 'Now what?' Shortplanks went after the con who told him how nice they were to eat, and asked him how to kill it. The con told planks, he would have to chop its head of with a sharp knife, and let it bleed, or the meat would be sour.

Planks went all over the wing, looking for a blade. There was plenty about, but who in there right mind was going to admit to having one.

Eventually planks got a blade. 'Now what?' By this time, planks had quite a small following of other planks.

One of them offered to hold the bird while planks gave it a chop on the neck, only planks missed, and hit the volunteers thumb.

The volunteer let go of the bird, and started howling. planks fell about laughing. So the volunteer smashed him in the mouth. So the brother of planks hit the volunteer in the mouth. The mate of the volunteer hit the brother. There was a right good punch up going on in the cell. A passing screw seeing the punch up pressed the panic button.

It happened that there was a dog handler on the landing. Him and his dog rushed towards the punch up. Just as they approached the planks cell, the pigeon flew out the cell door, half an inch above the dogs nose, and right between its ears.

The dog gave a primevel scream, a backward flip, and went straight between its handlers legs after the bird. The handler lost his grip.

The cons down the landing comeing out to see what the noise was about, saw a barking frenzied dog comeing at them, dived every which way, some over the rails into the safety netting, some straight up to grab the over head pipes. The pipes being red hot, and covered with years of dust, there grip lasted one second. They landed in horible heaps. Others dived for there cells, banging there doors so hard they busted right off there hinges.

Screws were pouring onto the wing from every direction. Cons on the upper landings, seeing this started throwing everything and anything, that was portable, – eggs, flour, water, furniture, you name it. Other cons having long standing grevences against other cons took advantage of the noise and confusion, to settle old scores. There was cuttings and stabbings, and fights just for the hell of it.

Screws who had been takeing a lot of shit, for a long time drew there sticks and started cracking heads. Any heads would do.

Well order was restored. Cons were draged of to segregation, the hospital. Screws seeing there chance of six months of, with full pay, developed severe shock disorders.

Shortplanks, well everybody knows he's too dumb to start, or take part in a riot. The next day he was seen putting fresh bread on his window sill. Roast pigeon was his 'dream'.

Soon the painters and decorators moved in. It was decided the filthy conditions were the cause of the riot.

And so life goes on. Its one hell of a ball.

T Shannon
TOM

133

Dear Tom,

When I got your letter from hospital, I rang the place up but they said they had discharged you already. I asked if you were alright and the man said 'Oh, we would never have discharged him if he hadn't been cured – if that's the right word.' This did not still my anxieties at all, and I was just wondering what to do next when two more letters from you reached me, almost together.

God, what a relief that it's over! And you won! But please be careful. The screws won't like it and will surely try to get their own back. I hope that, with such a victory behind you, you will feel able to show them a smiling face and not give them the opportunity.

Words fail me when I think about this affair. I had, of course, heard about shitty cells but had never been confronted and made to think about it. It is hard to know who to be most angry with – the screws, the governor, the con who did it. You had never done any of them any harm. What a mess we can make of things – and so unnecessarily. Just a bit of bloody-mindedness by someone and off we go, taking sides and waving our tribal totems without bothering to discover the truth of the matter.

It seems that in gaol, a new problem opens up as soon as an old one gets solved. I don't like the sound of the wing bully but I suppose you are used to that sort of thing. I hope I never am sent to gaol.

I'm warming to the idea of making a book out of your letters, but it wouldn't be my book but yours. Furthermore, I wouldn't dream of editing your letters. They are brilliant just as they are. Perhaps it would cause you trouble though, if it was published while you were still inside. And there are probably rules about prisoners writing about their experiences. I seem to remember reading somewhere that you're not even allowed to keep a diary.

Nor have I any idea how easy it would be to find a publisher but I think they ought to be published. These two letters alone have so much to offer the reader. An insight into what goes on in gaol, an unravelling of a crisis with a happy ending, a hilarious story (Short Planks) and a brilliant poem. I think 'Its a wee square world, is my world' is the best you've sent me yet.

About Fred, do not think I am prying. It must be difficult to think about let alone speak or write about it but if you do write to me about it, I want you to feel sure that I would not show it to anyone or speak about it unless you told me to. I say this because when I have a problem I do find it helps to write it all down and also to share it. Sometimes, just writing it down helps – and then tearing it up.

I think that girl on the cassette is a Swedish actress who played the role of Elvira Madigan in a film which used it as its musical theme. She's pretty, isn't she.

That Dr Khan sounds a good bloke. He showed all the others up. I'll be very interested to hear if you get anything back from Angela Rumbold or her staff. In the meanwhile, I was quite impressed with the reaction of the Prison Reform Trust. They gave good advice and offered to contact the prison governor, but I stopped them, fearing it might make your plight worse. In the meanwhile, I do think it is a good thing that we are writing to each other. All your letters got through without any interference. It means you are not totally isolated when there is a crisis although there isn't much I can do. But the fact may make the screws pause for thought.

We are very excited because a pair of mallard ducks are hanging around our new pond as if they intend to nest there. I do hope they do. It has made me modify my campaign against rabbits in the garden. The house is like a blockhouse in the Wild West, with loopholes in every direction so that if a rabbit strays too close, I can shoot him – or rather, at him. Unfortunately, neither of us likes to eat rabbit.

We're having a difficult spring on the farm because it's so cold and wet. We ought to be making our silage now but the forage harvester would just get bogged. Anyway, we'll have to let the grass dry out before we make it into silage. If not, it will give off effluent which is toxic to rivers. We daren't let it reach even a ditch. There is a £20,000 fine and I don't have that handy. But I fear the grass will be too old to make good silage. In the meanwhile, the corn's growing some splendid mildews and rusts but it will have a month or so to recover.

I am so, so happy that your latest ordeal is over. Let us hope it is the last.

Yours ever,
Chris

PS I took these pictures of some of the machines we use these days. Bit of a change since your farming days!

Dear Chriss

I don't have to write the address now that you have that booklet of prisons. I got another one.

Everything here is fine. I'v settled down now. I was moved to an even better cell, with a VIEW across the park.

I see all kinds of ducks, and wild birds, even phesents. With two very high fences around this place, it must be a safe place for birds, and of course with all the food that cons throw out the windows its party time for the local bird population.

To my left I can see a lake, and the patchwork fields of the farms.

Its the best view I'v ever had.

I'v got my cell spotless, and comfy.

The wings here are on the spur system, with 7 cells to the spur, so the noise level is a lot lower; in fact, very peacefull.

We get out to the park every weekend evening and sat and sunday morning, and afternoons. I do not do gym anymore, I just walk round and round the soccer field.

No trouble with bullies, and no job yet. I'v lost all my wages. £2.50 for the next month. So I'm a pounce, till I get a job, and start earning.

I'm surprised, that your surprised. I have a lady probation officer from birmingham. I'v lived in Brum for the last thirty years. My crime happened in shord end birmingham. I was tried at birmingham crown court. The probation officer comes to see me once a year. I always know when she is due as she always sends me a £10 gift before she comes.

She promises me the sky, and the moon and stars, when she is sitting talking to me. Then goes away and forgets me for another year, but I like her. She has a trim figure. I would not mind giveing her:- TUT, TUT, I have just finished reading Zorba the Greek, fantastic.

I have listened to the tapes you sent, but my brain is going haywire at a hundred miles an hour, because of no tobacco. My nerves are shattered, but time passes, so I'll get some snout soon enough. In the meanwhile, I'm glad I don't have a cat or I would be kicking it into touch. I don't have any mates here yet. I just can't be bothered. I can talk to you forever on paper. If we met in person, I would clamp up. I just dont know how to talk to people, in person.

It's nice you have some mallards. How are the crops coming on?

Its a shame you don't like rabbit to eat. There a good meal. If you shoot one on monday, cook it with is eyes in. Then it will see you through the week!! I have a window that's 43″ by 47″. Do you have a piece of spare cloth for a curtain please?

till again

T Shannon
TOM

Dear Chriss

Thank God, I got a smoke, at last. I got in a bit of debt, borrowing tobacco. But that's o.k.

My cell is eight feet, by 7'3", with a window I can sit at, and look out. Instead of having to stand on a table to look out.

In the last three prisons, Maidstone, Long lartin and Swaleside, we were encouraged to buy and wear any civvie clothes we liked, only to have them confiscated here.

This is because the P.O.A. have this place by the short and curlies, canteen mentality. But I like the situation of this prison. I have the best view, I'v ever had.

I think the wild birds have cottoned on to the fact that there are big security fences makeing the place secure from preditors.

I'm writing to the minister of prisons, to ask why we are encouraged to buy civvies in other nicks, only to have them taken from us here.

Radio reception here is terible, maybe its the huge fences.

I hope they will give me a job soon, so I can go on having tobacco.

Since I got here there's been a terrible wind blowing. Perhaps its because we are so close to the sea. This wind is starting to piss me off. There's no respite from it.

Nothing in prison buildings fits properly so the wind howels through all the cracks. It's like liveing in a cell full of banchees. The food here is excellent.

The only thing that mars this place is that we have an awfull lot of afro carrabeans. They seem to be unable to do anything without shouting.

It's as if they are all deaf. They will stand one foot from each other and shout. There favourite saying seems to be;

'Man me want, Man me want.'

I like to see the afros playing soccar. They do get stuck in. The ones that are not on the ball, will stand and shout at those who are. There all managers.

Can you explane to me why someone (myself) who does nothing all day, every day, can be so weary, so tired all the time?

I have about as much energy as a spent pencil battery, and crushing headaches, that drive me to distraction.

If you are getting this wind, I hope its not flattening your crops.

There are ducks here that are a light dun colour. I wonder what kind they are?

As there are no toilets in these cells, you get a lot of shit parcels thrown out the windows. This is just lazyness, as we can get out of our cells at night. There is a panal inside each cell. You press the button 'go' and an amber light comes on. When it switches to green, you open your door, and go. Then when you return to your cell, you look into a small window that gives you a series of numbers. You press the buttons that correspond to these numbers, and the cell door locks. You are allowed six minutes out of your cell. If you take longer they shout over the intercom;- 'SHANNON RETURN TO YOUR CELL.' All computer controled.

I'm a tea addict, so I have to empty my piss pot once anight.

We also have two locks on our doors. One that can only be locked or opened by the screws, and one that we have the key to.

Most of the cell here is taken up with the bed and, the locker unit, leaving about three and a half feet of space to move about in.

I think the trouble with these old P.O.A. members is that years ago you had to stand to attention when they spoke to you, and call them sir. They could take you down to the strip cells and rip your clothes off you, then maim and kill you, and have it whitewashed in the courts. There power over cons was tremendous. They are reluctant to let go of these powers. Since the onset of Maggie Thatcher's fresh start, when there massive overtime was taken from them, they have fought against every humanistic change in the system. In the canteen mentality we are all animals, not worthy of decent treatment.

It was very decent of you to try and help my confrontation with the bully boys here. All I wanted was a clean cell. I think it was my two letters to the minister of prisons, that led to my getting a clean cell. Even then I washed the walls, and scrubbed the floor.

I have always been known for keeping my cell spotless. After all I have to live in it.

Except for writing to you through the prison reform trust, I know nothing about them. There are a few such organisations of this type. They are not any good at helping the individual. I think they just hold there hands out for government grants.

There was one group N.A.G.R.O., who used to send lifers a ten pound grant every year for hobbies. I think they went broke. I used to write to Amnesty International telling them all the wrongs that happen in prison, but I lost there address. I will come across there address again. In the meantime, life is a ball,

Yours
T Shannon
TOM

c/o Prison Reform Trust
59 Caledonian Road
N1 9BU

20th June 1993

Dear Tom,

I'm afraid I've been a bit slow and have two letters of yours to answer. I have an excuse. We've been hard at it in the fields making silage (rather late) and hay (rather early). Normally these crops come a few days apart but this year is all upside down because of the late spring. Having them come together has made it a bit hectic and bad-tempered. When we stop each day, usually after sunset, I don't feel very energetic. You're not the only one I've stood up.

Even so, it feels good to have our winter feed in the barn. The beasts won't starve. It is always a good moment. The hay is very good and smells lovely. It is the reward of hours of hand tedding to tease out the green bits. I'm not too confident about the silage. Good silage should make a good smell too. Ours doesn't smell at all this year. I suspect it did not get enough sun. It is all slush and fibre with no sugars or proteins to make it ferment properly – or to give it any feed value. Still, we'll see.

I enclose one of your envelopes. Unless this is how you sent it, it seems that someone has tampered with it. I thought you ought to know though I can't imagine that it will influence what you say!

In the meanwhile, Ann and I have continued to rejoice that everything has turned out so well for you after all. Maybe this horrible shitty cell business will prove a turning point. Having won such a victory, you can afford to be magnanimous and show a smiling face. In all your crises this year, you have been vindicated, and it is a long time since you had an adjudication or a knock-back. If you can avoid one until your next LRC, maybe you will find yourself on the slipway towards release.

And the normal circumstances at Blundeston seem good. You've got a room with a view, good food, a low noise level. If it wasn't for all the other cons and the screws, it would be like a holiday camp – at least relative to some other gaols you have known (and possibly to some holiday camps!) Just as well – you have some recuperating to do.

It must be interesting to watch all those ducks. I love ducks. I enclose a chart to help you identify them. In the meanwhile, I'm afraid those broody mallards have thought better of using our pond for their nest. Can't blame them – it's still very bare. In the meanwhile, a pair of grey wagtails have taken up residence which is almost as good.

I hope to God you get a job soon. There's only one thing more soul destroying than idleness and that is idleness without any tobacco. It's no substitute, but I have sent you a book of poetry. I hope this won't embarrass you! I have recently taken up learning four lines of poetry a day. I think you like poetry and might enjoy doing the same. It helps me cling onto the hope that I'm not yet brain-dead.

Also, when I wake at night and my mind is haunted with unwelcome thoughts, I find I can drive them away by rehearsing all the poetry I have learned – which usually puts me back to sleep again anyway. Try it. The anthology I've sent was by General Wavell. He only included poems he knew by heart.

I've also sent some curtain material. There is more than you need but it was left over from some curtains Ann made years ago and is of no use to us. You can sell what you can't use.

Just to make you mad with envy, I'm off to Scotland for a week's fishing soon. I may not write for a bit.

Yours ever,
Chris

P.S. Did you hear that story about Dorothy Parker? When she was told that President Hoover had died, she asked – 'How could they tell?'

FIVE

THE CENSOR

Dear Chriss

What a pathetic team, England put up against Norway. Two-Nil. What happens in a prison, when England plays any team, and it's on the radio. When englands scores, every con pounds his door. It sounds like a two minute thunder clap.

But when England lose you can cut the silence with a knife. It's as if the whole prison is embarrast. 'After that performance we are.' One of our teams could have done better. I can't see past the prison fence tonight. There's a very heavy mist. I'v never seen so many ducks, and other water fowl, as there are out there tonight. I wonder if they are scared of what might be out there in the mist.

I think you should put a time capsule under ground, somewhere on your farm. If you put it in one of those thick plastic bags sucking all the air out of it, in many years to come some historian will thank you. 'Don't I write some drivel.'

I'm banged up twenty two hours a day, as I don't have a job yet, so I'm not wise to this place yet.

4-6-93

I dont know what's going on here with me. I'm just left banged up all day. I get unlocked at 7-30 in the morn, for slop out, breakfast. Then banged up at 9.00 till 10.30. Sometimes they forget to unlock me at 10.30, so I have to press the call button, at eleven to get my half hour exercise and lunch.

At twelve, I'm banged up till 1.30, for slop out, then banged up at 2.00 till 3.30, again if they remember me.

Dinner is at four, then bang up from 5oc till six. At approx 6.15, we get out to the field till 7.15. Then bang up at 8oc till 7.30 next morning.

At 6oc in evening if you don't want to go out to the field you can watch a video, or play pool. The pool cues are only four feet long. Any longer and you would hit the walls, when taken a stroke. The video costs us 25p per week.

As there are 63 cons on this wing that's £15.75 per week? 'I hope. I'm no good at sums.'

There are seven wings. One wing has two cons per cell, and another has four cons per cell, but I don't know how many cells on those wings, yet.

The television room is kept locked all day till six o clock in the evening, and the pool room, and I just seen in the papers that the cons get too much T.V. The gullible public, reading the sun, or other papers and believing all they read, then screaming for all these luxuries to be stopped because crime is getting more violent.

Well I got news for the british public. It's going to get worse. Even in prison, cons are getting mugged and burgled, and its all down to DRUG'S. That's why I hide my sony tape machine, every time I leave my cell, (and I have a key).

The reason drug addicts burgle, mug, sell there bodys, and a whole host of other crimes is because, they have stolen everything that moves in there own homes, allienating there whole familys. There familleys breath a sigh of relief when they are put away, for a sentence. The longer the better, I bet.

If I left my cell door open, I would only need two lines of this page, to tell you what was left when I returned. They know what would happen if they are caught cell theiving, but they are desparate for DRUG'S. And there is no shortage in prison, no shortage at all, 'just a shortage of funds.'

The city addicts are now crawling up motorways, in search for easy pickings. With drug addicts, and P.O.A. intransigents, prison is HELL. 'What is it like out there'?

5-6-93

I have just been informed, I am to start work in the print shop.

148

I have been talking to a lad that worked in the print shop at maidstone. He tells me there is no work in the print shop here. Everyone just sits around, drinking tea, and smoking.

The weekend starts tomorrow, and we get two and a half hours, outside, on saturday and sunday. The government has decreed we should be unlocked for no less than twelve hours per day. The P.O.A. and its members have said, No. We the cons are the captive punchbags in this on going dispute between the government and the P.O.A.

13-6-93

I have been on segregation since 7th.

I refused to hand my letters into the office opened. Censorship has been stopped, but the P.O.A. millitants here, backed by the Govenor, who would rather kiss the P.O.A. ass, than stand up for the rights of the cons. Also in other prisons, they allow us to wear any or all the civie clothes we have. Here they only allow us two t shirts.

The government has stated that all cons are to be unlocked for twelve hours, per day. Again the p.o.a. are saying, no.

It was probably a P.O.A. millitent who opened that letter, but I cant prove it, so!

I intend to stay on the seg, till I'm moved. I have written to the Min for prisons, as I'v had no answers. I can only gess the P.O.A. have garbaged my letter's.

I wonder if this one will reach you?

I'm happy you got good silage in, I hope you get another good crop or two,

I'v heard about that mildue, and rust. Will the wheat be compleatly lost? I hope not.

16-6-93

I quiet like it here on solitary. No hassle from other cons, the peace and quiet is marvelous. I think, I may spend a year or so on the seg. I will get moved from here in a few months.

I just found out, the No 1 govenor has only been here a

month. Aprently he was a soliciter, or a barrester. All the cons say there was a woman govenor here before him, and the place was great. I think what happened was, this govenor arrived brand new and the P.O.A. militants jumped on his inexperience, and graudully clamped down on the privalages the old govenor allowed.

The fact that they can cock a snoot at the government's recommendations that we can wear civies, that there can be no more cencering, and no extensions of unlock. I think the P.O.A. militants have convinced the new govenor, that if he gives us an inch, we will take a mile.

Of course there will always be those who will, but most of us just want to do our porridge, and get out. Any cons biggest enemy is his fellow cons. Those screws, that realise, that none of us want to be here, just get on with there jobs, without fuss. Other screws blame the cons for everything that's wrong, like the bad brick layer, blames the bricks, or a slow ditch digger blames the shovel.

All, or nearly all, my ajudications are because I refuse as an individule to give in to those P.O.A. intransagents, or could not care less, lethargic P.O.A. members who are just killing time. The trouble is a lot of young screws are swayed by the canteen mentately of these older screws.

The Goverment is activelly encourageing young screws to join the new screws union. The older screws hold all the top jobs:- Principle officers, senior officers, and the used to be chiefs are all now assistent Govs. But the young screws are, (some of them) career minded and climbing there way up the ladder, (good luck to them).

Some of the older generation of screws still hanker after the days when they could batter, maim, and kick the cons to death. They knew they would get a white wash in any court. Law breakers will always blame everybody, and anybody, for the reasons they commit there crimes, and when they are punished they will scream, blue murder. They think if they could get away with it outside, they should have the same privalige inside. They can't seem to understand that they are being punished for the crimes they done. They think society is just having a go at them. So they sit and plan bigger and better ways to hit back at society. In these places they learn how.

There's a young lad on the seg with me. His two brothers are convicts, his sister, and father are cons. It costs the tax payers a fortune, in inter prison visits, for them to see each other. 'AH WELL'

Gods Blood, I do go on a bit.

So you cant afford £20,000 polution fines, and here's me thinking I'd latched on to a Millionair. 'Aint life a Beech',

T Shannon
TOM

P.S. TO GET BEATTING BY AMERICA?

151

23-6-93

Dear Chriss

What a book to send to a prisoner, beautiful, wonderful. 'Thank you so much.' I had a lump in my throat, finding old favourites, and lots of new ones to come, I bet.

What a title, Other Men's Flower's, right on the nose. I was in a bar called the wreckers, in the rock hotel, rock cornwall, many years ago. Someone asked me what I was doing in that part of the country, and I just up and spoke Masefield's, sea fever. I suddenly relized the bar had gone quiet, and everyone was listening to me. It left me with a queer feeling, and about three or four pints in front of me, and a red face. I will treasure, I do already treasure, Other Men's Flower's. 'Thank you,'

I have not seen the cloth yet, as we are not allowed curtains on the block.

I'd forgotten I'd asked for that. The screw who brought the property book, for me to sign, said it was very good stuff, and more than enough. Thank you, again.

I'v had all my hair off, and beard. I don't have access to all the soap and water I would like on the seg, so its easier to keep clean, if you have your hair off, till I get out of this mess.

I just lay here twenty three hours a day, so I wont write my usual volumes. No input, no output. So I'll send one of the flowers back to you.

T Shannon
TOM

Farmers
Man to the plough,
Wife to the cow,
Girl to the yarn,
Boy to the barn,
and your rent will be netted;
           BUT
Man tally-ho,
Miss piano,
Wife silk and satin
Boy greek and latin
And youll soon be Gazetted.
           ANON.

Dear Chriss

So it's off fishing, in the land of the dry land kilted submarine corp. I'm filled with envy.

I don't know if I thanked you for the three pictures of the farm machines.

I'm on the seg for refusing to take up the job they gave me in the print shop here.

I refused the job as a protest againnst cencoring my letters, and for confiscating my civie clothes, plus the atmosphere is horrible. It is a pity, as this place is beautifuly situated.

I won't put up with intransagent, bloody minded P.O.A. bullies. We cons did not instacate fresh start. We did not take away there massive overtime earnings. It was the Thatcher Government. If these people, the P.O.A. and its members, have greavences, let them go on strike, and get it over with. And stop using us as there captive punchbags.

'Zut Alors'

To come from a place like maidstone, where your on first name terms with the screws, play pool with them, or cards, and football, then come to a regime, that wants to rule with a big stick. 'Fuck um'

I know, I have at least seven more years to do. I won't do them under the heel of other peoples discontent. Some Govenors are now saying in public in the media, to the P.O.A. members;- 'Do your Jobs, or leave the service.' I wish they would. Now that I'v got that off my chest. I say chest, because mine is so sunk, you would need a good miner to find it.

I look like one of those people you see in movies about jewish prisoners, in nazi camps. 'God bless them.' I have a feeling, (perhaps not in our lifetimes, but mabey.) that the next great war this country gets into will be with france, and germany. France is becomeing very dictatorial towards us. And they – France and Germany – are ripping us off financialy.

I watch great lorry loads of produce comeing into prisons, and all of it french or spanish. Don't our country produce fruits and veg anymore.

26-6-93

(later)

A youngster here told me of a stamp saving scam. You rub your stamp with wax. Then, when it comes to me or you, we just rub the postal mark off and reuse the stamp. I'v rubbed this stamp. Try it. 'Shsss'

27-6-93

6.57 oc P.M. There's very little disturbance in solitary, on Sunday afternoons, (Just the way I like it). So I relaxed and listened to Mozart. 'Yes I do like it', and Schubert.

One Golden Opera, and one Beethoven;- My favourite. Thats five all told. If you come across one of classic guitar, but not John Williams, he's too stuffy, I would be very apreceative. I heard a lady Guitarist playing alhambra, but I missed her name. Typicle.

Don't tell me any more about your fishing trip. I'll just weep with envy, I'll now listen to EINE KLEINE NACHT-MUSIK, and conduct the bricks.

Yours T Shannon
TOM

29 June 1993

Dear Tom,

Three of your letters, one a multiple, arrived just after I had left home so Ann sent them up here. Sorry about the odd bits of paper I'm using to reply.

Oh Tom! Are you ever going to get out of gaol? I blame myself. It was stupid to send you that envelope. I might have known you'd make it a matter of honour. I know the screws are wrong to censor letters but the law does allow them a little discretion still. I agree, they probably abuse it. Ann's con in Wakefield has all his letters censored (and apparently hers too which makes her very cross). She wrote to our MP but he merely sent her a standard reply from the Home Office implying that it was done for the sake of the prisoner, to prevent him from committing a folly – like topping himself.

Ann's con feels much the same as you about it and about screws in general but he handles it differently from you. He reckons screws want to provoke cons and, if one reacts, it makes their day. He reacts with a superior smile and hopes to irritate them that way. I don't know what this guy did. He doesn't seem like a professional crook but I think it must have been quite impressive. When he had to go into hospital recently, they gave him a permanent escort of two screws beside his bed – day and night.

The fishing is lousy – so far one small farmed fish between the three of us. They say that the sand eels which salmon eat when they leave the river have been over-fished and that most of the young salmon starve. I have heard that the Danes run their power stations on fuel made of sand eels but I expect that it's just a scare story. Whatever the reason, the salmon don't seem to come back to the rivers any more – at least not this one!

Still – all is not lost! Fishing is also about the open air, the dappled mountains, the dippers and the wagtails and the swirling, soothing stream.

Last word, while space remains. Do please think again about your protest. Maybe it's just what the screws want you to do. Please don't make their day!

Yours ever,
Chris

c/o Prison Reform Trust
59 Caledonian Road
N1 9BU

8th July 1993

Dear Tom,

I'm back at the farm. I would have written earlier but when I got back, I found them resurfacing our lane and offering road planings cheap. I have got a track which I badly wanted to surface so I accepted their offer with both hands even though it meant clearing all sorts of stuff out of the way to make it possible, preparing the surface and then spreading several tons by hand daily. Thus – frenetic activity.

Among other things, I had to move a large compost heap that was in the way. I started to do this with the foreloader of the tractor and disturbed a large grass snake which was in it. It was a lovely snake which I have seen many times around the garden. I hope I did not harm her for I discovered soon that she had been in the act of laying her eggs. There were about thirty of them in a big clump, leathery and the size of small bantams' eggs.

We have decided to adopt her children. I could not leave them where they were but we have divided them into three groups. We've put one into another compost heap, one into our hot cupboard and one into a glass tank beside a storage heater. According to our books, it will be at least six weeks before they hatch out. I'll keep you posted.

We used to keep snakes – anything from grass snakes to boa-constrictors, provided they were not poisonous. We had an asthmatic son who could not tolerate any pet with fur or feathers. Snakes make lovely easy pets. They rarely eat, as seldom shit, don't need walks but just to be handled, which is enjoyable – sinuous and rather sexy. Even so, we had plenty of adventures with them, like the time one of the boa-constrictors got loose. It decided to take refuge on my bicycle, threading itself in and out of the spokes of the front wheel. It took us hours to get it free. They are quite strong. At one time we thought we'd have to send for International Rescue.

One Autumn evening, my daughter and her boy friend were driving through London with a python in a hatbox when they decided to go window-shopping in Kensington Church Street, forgetting to secure the lid. Of course, when they got back – no python. They searched the car and were rootling through the piles of fallen leaves outside when a policeman arrived. Told the problem, he completely lost his head, blowing his whistle, trying to levitate and shoo away the passers by. From a respectful distance, he ordered them to find the snake but they searched and searched but to no avail. They decided it must have gone down a drain. They like dark places. At last, he calmed down and let them leave.

It wasn't down a drain. In the following spring when the weather warmed up, we realized that it was still somewhere in the car but dead. We never discovered its hiding place but it took two years for the smell to die away.

No news from you. I hope this means good news but I doubt it. Last time you went off the air, someone had stabbed your spleen. I hope it's not anything like that!

Yours ever,
Chris

PS I tried to rub the post mark off that stamp but most of the Queen came off too.

15th July 1993

Dear Tom,

Another week and no letter from you. My mind is ranging over all the possible reasons. Is it this censorship business? Perhaps you are refusing to write while they continue to censor your letters. I can see it might be hard for either side to back down. In case this is the problem, I enclose a few stamped postcards which might help break the deadlock. By their nature they are open and read by everyone. You might use one at least to let me know what the trouble is.

In the meanwhile, I have been toying with the idea of contacting the Prison Reform Trust or your Probation Officer to see if they can help unravel the problem. I hesitate, however, since there may not be a problem and then I'd feel foolish for stirring things up! Maybe you just don't feel like writing at the moment. I will wait a bit longer.

Perhaps I am enlarging things in my mind because we've been having one of our periodical rows on the farm. They only seem to happen once every five years or so. Then someone goes too far – or at least, I think so and then things are very unpleasant and tense for a few days until we all return to our attitudes of mutual trust and respect.

I have finished making the track. I flattened it with a vibrating plate but then got the road gang to bring along their roller. I am glad it's done. It was too much like hard work. Still, I'm rather proud of it.

I heard a statistic on the radio today. Apparently 70% of all cons were brought up by only one parent (or, like you, none). And yet the tendency today seems to be almost to encourage single women to have babies. I believe something like half the country's children have only one active parent. I don't advocate a Victorian attitude to fallen women but the consequences for the future are alarming. I keep thinking of that Greek who said 'whom the Gods would destroy, they first make mad.'

Please use one of these cards.

Yours ever,
Chris

PS Also enclosed is a small bag of smelly things – thyme, chamomile, lavender, rosemary. They come from what we call our fragrant bank, (inspired by Midsummer Night's Dream – 'I know a bank where the wild thyme blows, etc'). It is a lovely place to lie on a hot day. I thought these might bring a whiff of outdoors to the seg.

c/o Prison Reform Trust
59 Caledonian Road
N1 9BU

22nd July 1993

Dear Tom,

Another week and still nothing. I am getting seriously worried. Saying poetry to myself at night is beginning to work less well! Luckily we've been working hard all day because the barley has come early and so I haven't had time to start ringing up the Prison Reform Trust, etc.

I still am hesitating anyway. I might just add to your problems which, when you last wrote, seemed heavy enough for the time being. I don't want to stir things without your prior agreement or even knowing whether there is a problem.

Are you getting my letters, I wonder. Perhaps you've been ghosted. If so – three cheers! Blundeston hasn't been your best experience to date!

Yours ever,
Chris

PS Barley came off quite well despite early anxieties.

Dear Chriss

It's one hell of a job to get up the energy to write.

I'm listening to country, and western Now, if those people can put so much energy into so much garbage, surely, I can find some energy to put down a few words.

I expect to move soon. Where? I don't know yet. I'll let you know, as soon as it happens.

I got your letter with the smelly stuff, and your last letter with the stamped cards, and envelopes. 'Thank you'

I turn on the radio, turn it off, pick up a book, put it down.

I count the bricks, reach a total and start again.

I build fantistic constructions on the ceiling.

I sleep from twelve till two, from four thirty till six then from ten, till seven thirty in the morning,

'Now thats lathegy'.

I will bounce back to my usual gregarious penmanship, as soon as I get out of the segregation doldrums.

There would not be a lot of use in your going to bat for me, (a generious offer).

These organisations like the prison reform trust, are good at waffle for the media. As for helping individule inmates, there crap. I never heard of them, till I saw there advert for pen friends. I answered there advert, asking for a lady about my own age. They wrote back saying they were not a dating agency. I did write at the time I was serving life, so even if they were a dating agency, how could I have kept a date. Anyway you turned up, and it all worked out fine.

It sounds like things got a bit hectic and heated down there on the farm. I hope all is peaceful now.

If anyone deserves peace, its you, after your full and busy life.

I heard a sad report on the radio. Hill farmers commiting suiside. That's horrible. I worked for a few hill farmers in my itinerant days. There good people.

I hope your grandkids are not tireing you and Ann out.

My Regards
T Shannon TOM

25th July 1993

Dear Tom,

Your letter arrived today to my considerable relief. Thank God, I never stirred things up. I would have felt a fool.

It is depressing that you're still in seg. But the movement of letters is obviously ok, which is good. On the other hand, I am a bit worried about this lethargy. (I'm an enthusiastic worrier – ask my children!) I could have understood it in mid-June when you'd just come out of your hunger strike and all that confrontation over the shitty cell, but your letters then were frequent and full of life.

It's not sedatives, is it? I imagine the hours in seg might seem shorter if they were drowsier. Could it even be that you are being given sedatives without your knowledge – to keep you quiet? Either way, if there is any truth in it, I think it's very dangerous. A month is quite enough to get addicted.

Don't bother to write at any length if you don't feel like it but I would be grateful for an answer to two questions.

Question A – Are you on sedatives? – yes/no

Question B – If so, is it voluntary? – yes/no

All you need to do is quote the letter and put the answer on a postcard.

I won't bore you with too much about us in this letter. The barley came off quite well. About two and a half tons per acre which is rather good for us. A nice clean sample too, with a good bushel weight. We had a few interruptions for rain, but it went quite well. Can't complain. (You see! We don't always grumble!)

We held one of our furniture repair courses this week. Did

I ever tell you about them? We hold six a year in an unused outhouse where we've set up a workshop. We have a clientele of about 20 people who like to come and spend a weekend repairing their own furniture under the supervision of an expert (not us). It's good fun and very interesting. We nearly always have to turn away some of the applicants. We've only room for eight but luckily they don't all want to come at the same time.

Yours ever
Chris

c/o Prison Reform Trust
59 Caledonian Road
N1 9BU

5th August 1993

Dear Tom,

Still no answer about the matter of sedatives. I am afraid I
did something you may resent. I rang up the Probation
Office in Birmingham and got in touch with Jean.

I liked her very much. I think you're lucky to have such a
good friend. She said she'd seen you in mid-June and had
been impressed at how cheerful you were. She had not heard
that you've since gone back into seg. She is convinced that
you will not be getting sedatives without your knowledge or
against your will. Apparently that is totally illegal so perhaps
your fears about liquid coshes are unnecessary. It seems that
my worst fears were unnecessary too. If you're getting sedatives it's because you want them. I gather Jean is planning
another visit and will ring me afterwards.

Things are a bit hung up at the farm. The wheat looks
good and is ready for the combine but it keeps raining. I
hope it doesn't bring back the mildew which had cleared up
quite well. That happened last year. We had what looked like
a lovely crop ready for the combine on 4th August but the
combine driver asked our permission to delay a day so that
he could get in someone's oats. Well, oats are more vulner-
able to delay than wheat so we agreed. It rained next day and
nearly every day for six weeks. It cost us about half the crop.
I hope the guy's oats were good!

Hoping to hear from you soon.

Yours ever,
Chris

Dear Chriss

I can assure you, I'm not on any medication of any kind. In all my time in prison, I have managed to stay away from medication.

My lathergy is brought about simply because I'm banged up twenty three hours a day, sometimes twenty four when I can't be bothered with the one hour exercise.

I do get through a tremendous amount of books. Your small sony machine is a god send,

I was told on the 2-8-93 that I was going to swaleside on 3-8-93 but, I was told today, when all packed and ready, that I would not be going to swaleside after all.

I have just been told, I'm going to albany, on the Isle of Wight. When? I don't know yet. Albany has a terrible reputation, within the system. I prefare that kind of prison, where you know it's every man for himself. Where you are liable to get a kicking from cons or screws, but at least you know where you stand. I'v become an expert at walking mine fields of human aggreshion.

I have not had a shave since I was blocked so I resemble a skinny yeti.

I only go out on exersise when the sun shines and then I only sit in the corner of the yard and let the sun burn me, so I have quite a tan.

I wish I was with you getting the harvest in, but, I don't suppose its the same as I remember it, with those combine machines. It made me happy to know you are getting a good crop. I did worry if the weather would let up long enough, to allow the harvest to be got in.

Well just the mention of my moveing has cheered me up.

I'll soon be back in the letter writing business.

I'm told if I get a high cell in albany I will be able to see the seas, sailing boats and girls in swim suits.

'Girls' what are those?

Aint life an eye's delight.

Next one from next place
I hope, Yours Aye
T Shannon
TOM

c/o Prison Reform Trust
59 Caledonian Road
N1 9BU

8th August 1993

Dear Tom,

Your letter arrived today to my relief. It seems I've been shying at shadows again.

I think I can imagine how energy-sapping seg must be. I can't handle not being busy. My life is like a bicycle. As soon as it slows down, I start wobbling. I'm sure many people are like me. The idleness of prison must destroy them.

I am terribly pleased to hear that you will be moving soon. Blundeston has been one long horror story. Almost anywhere must be better. Perhaps Albany is better than its reputation. I dare say the screws there are hoping the same applies to you!

Even so, should you not be doing something to get yourself a bit fitter? You must have got a bit flabby in all these weeks in seg. Shouldn't you be preparing to confront a new set of cons? If they behave anything like our cattle do with a newcomer, you'll need to be able to account for yourself.

I know it can't be easy slammed up all day but maybe you could do some exercises. Back in the seventies, I began to find that I was getting flabby and my back was hurting after a bout of hard work so I've done exercises every day since. They take about ten minutes and I really HATE them but I do them every day. One missed day and I would never get them going again.* And they work. All the aches and pains have disappeared and I am really quite fit for my age. Farm

---

*Actually, I haven't done them every day. I have a few 'escape routes'. If I get up before 6am, I excuse myself, or if I'm in too small a room. Also, if I'm up after midnight, I'm allowed to do next morning's exercises before going to bed. For some reason they are easier then.

work, garden work, much bicycling and even some quite violent sports. I'll send you a description of my routine if you like, but you would know what you need to do without any advice from me.

We've got the wheat in but still have some 1500 bales of straw to carry. The bloody rain is holding us up. It'll be making them heavier too!

Yours ever,
Chris

c/o Prison Reform Trust
59 Caledonian Road
N1 9BU

21st August 1993

Dear Tom,

All the straw is in so the farm year is about complete (except for the accounts). We can face the winter reasonably sure that we won't run short of food even if the silage quality is not particularly fattening. We won't know, of course, until we open up the clamp and we've got about 70 big bales of the stuff to feed before then. I think the bales will be better than the clamp. They had more sun.

It's raining again today. I've just been round the cattle, all huddled and miserable in the corners of their fields. Unbelievably, since it's still August, they are showing signs of cutting up the fields.

Apart from that, a wet day suits me. I have so many indoor things to catch up on – like this letter. It's nice to have an opportunity to stay indoors without feeling guilty. I was brought up to feel that it was rather decadent to be indoors when the sun was shining – ought to be out in the fresh air (there was some in those days)! I suppose farming hasn't helped. If the sun's shining, I feel I ought to be out looking for some hay to make.

I enclose a magazine the Prison Reform Trust has produced about their penfriend scheme. They asked me to contribute. I'm afraid my effort looks very stiff and reserved beside some of the others – but then you and I are not the flirtatious types. To be honest, I'm rather disturbed to see how intimate some of the lady penfriends have become with their cons. One has even married the bloke! To do something so fundamental on such an artificial relationship! Perhaps

I'm just showing my age thinking of it as fundamental. I'm afraid it's going to fuel your regrets about that young blond penfriend you asked for!

Several of the cons in it are obviously on the countdown to release which made me think about your impending LRC – in September I think. I do hope it goes well. In the meanwhile, I suppose you're still counting the bricks, getting flabbier and hairier. I had a beard for about twenty years. I think I grew it so as not to be typed. I cut it off when it was quite white and made me look like a stupid old goat. That was a trauma! I hadn't seen my face for all that time -- talk about Dorian Gray. I'll never forget Ann's look of apprehension as I emerged from the bathroom.

What news of the move?

Yours ever,
Chris

PRISON REFORM TRUST ARTICLE

My wife and I have each been writing to a prisoner for about a year. We had not realized that the PRT's penfriends scheme was hardly any older but we have no doubt that whoever first thought of it had a brilliant idea. Perhaps it is because we were rather early recruits to the scheme that the Trust has asked me to write something about it – preferably something funny.

Now, I believe rather passionately that it is our duty to be as funny as possible, as much of the time as possible. The graver the problem, the more important it is to be funny about it and laugh – or so I thought. Actually, I don't want to be funny about my correspondence with Tom. Perhaps it is one of the great successes of the penfriends scheme that it momentarily persuades incorrigibly frivolous people like me to be serious.

I say this with a sense of great humility. A year ago, I would never have imagined that I could so much look forward to a letter from a stranger inhabiting a world so foreign to my own. Nor would I have believed that my own letters, so vapid and uninspired, could come to mean so much to him. It is a sobering experience. My wife and I seem to have involved ourselves in something at which we simply must not fail.

It is, of course, a little eery – like speaking to sailors trapped in a sunken submarine. It is contact with a world cut off, a strange and terrible world, for which many able people are seeking a better solution. Let us hope that they find one. In the meanwhile, we, who do not aspire to solve it, can at least bring a little hope and humanity into the life of someone entrammelled by it. And, if we do, we will find that he or she will bring something into our own life, entrammelled as it too is by a host of everyday pursuits. Are we not lucky that we can choose them?

And if enough people do so, is it possible that their combined efforts might actually modify the system which has so far defied so many well meaning reforms? If every prisoner could be provided by this means with a window on an outside where less brutal values still exist, might those which do exist inside not be softened or, at least, made more resistable?

SIX

ALBANY

21-8-93

Dear Chriss

I'm of to albany 24th Tuesday.

I'm happy you got your wheat in.

I hope you will forgive me for the shortness of these letters. It's so difficult to get the brain in gear, with this 24 hour long bang up. Life is extremly eneventful, when you only have the four walls to argue with.

I will go to albany, and be goody, goody 'I hope'.

There I go, staring at this paper.

I will write from albany, after a week or two.

We can only write about WHAT goes on in our surroundings, as nothing is happening around me for the last nine weeks, I hope you can see the problem.

Let's see what albany brings.

Yours till Albany
T Shannon
TOM

c/o Prison Reform Trust
59 Caledonian Road
N1 9BU

23rd August 1993

Dear Tom,

Your letter about the move has just come and I'm writing post haste to welcome you to Albany. I hope, I <u>hope</u>, I HOPE it will be better than Blundeston. It must be. Nothing could be worse. I guess the first few days will show.

It will probably help that you have no high expectations. I often find that something I'm looking forward to disappoints while things I'm dreading turn out to be quite fun. It's all in the mind, of course. And I'm not suggesting that Albany will be fun. It's not meant to be fun.

Did I ever tell you about General Veresz? He was a friend of my father's before the war. During the war, he commanded the Hungarian army fighting the Russians and, when the Russians won, he was put in gaol. He stayed there for 12 years until the 1956 uprising enabled him to escape to England. His 12 years were divided into three equal parts. The first four years, he was in a big cell with all sorts of other important people – generals, ministers, bishops, ambassadors, judges and so forth. Then he spent four years in solitary. Finally he shared a cell for four years with a peasant.

He told us that the worst period was the first – watching all these eminent men falling to bits until they were actually fighting each other for the last bun. He spent his four years solitary trying to recall all the poetry he had ever learned. To his own amazement, he finished up with nearly a bookful, like General Wavell. Eventually he was dredging things up that he had completely forgotten ever learning. The last period was the best. The two men were so different that they did not quarrel. The peasant taught him everything he knew about growing vines and making wine. Veresz taught him everything about Napoleon's campaigns.

I'm not sure why I'm telling you about Veresz now. It would have been more useful three months ago!

Good luck at Albany!

Yours ever,
Chris

PS I've been thinking more and more about this idea of trying to publish your letters. Are you sure it won't make life even harder for you and cause you trouble with the screws? Think very carefully and let me know if you really want me to go on.

26-8-93

Dear Chriss

I got here at 12oc today. I stayed two nights at Wandsworth. Pure hell.

I was just under 3 months on segregation at Blund. If only I was not so pig headed, and if P.O.A. bullies could be sorted out. Ah well that's all behind me. I dont have time to myther over it, its done.

I got your letter as soon as I got here sent on from blundeston. Now that was a real treat, to arrive at a strange prison, and have a friendly letter handed to me.

You were scathing about the weather when the wheat was in the fields. Now it's in, your saying the rain is not a bad thing, God must be having a fit trying to please you.

Well I'm five hours into this place, I arrived with heart thumping, choaked with apprenshion, ready to silently scream my way into another hell.

But, what a difference. The screws on reception were as good as I'v ever seen screws. My cell is newly furbished, beautifully painted, spotless, with everything I need inside. As for the rest of it, I'll tell you when I find out.

The radio reception on F.M. is marvelous. The stereo is great. I don't think I'll ever stop praseing my walkman, for sound production. I borrowed two batteries for it as I don't get paid till saturday. £2.50 unemployment. I'm gasping for a smoke but thats nothing new. I hope I get a job soon.

I'll tell you about my future when I'v met and talked to the welfare and probation here.

As my introduction to this place was very humane, then I shall be very coopertive. Forgive my spelling – Thesaurus gone adrift.

'Classic F.M. comeing through great.' Listening as I write. The laughing song, by flog a mouse, I think. Sound the trumpet, beautiful.

Well, I'm off again, writing I mean.

I'm nackered with three days getting here,

I shall pray, to God, to keep me on an even keel, so I can sail off this Island, to a better future some day I hope.

Never mind the rain. Get your wet gear on, and get those hundreds of jobs done.

Despite all the motorways, 'England looks lovely'. The sun shone for me all the way, and I saw two Magpies. Wonder what that means. I saw a horse box on its side, on the london orbital. The driver was taken away in an ambulance. The horse was still in the box, poor horse.

soon again,
T Shannon
TOM

Sat 28TH

Dear Chriss

Got your wellcoming letter today. I don't mind if you print
any of my letters. Once they land on your door step they are
your property. If anyone is dumb enough to pay cash money
for them, I'll have some by all means. It would go into my
private cash fund which is empty.

I could then buy batteries, and steradent to clean my false
teeth, and some shampoo. There is some thing that you
could look for me, and that's a half tin, or a small container
to keep my rolling tobacco in.

I have a 2oz old holborn tin. It's too large and thick. If you
know someone who smokes a pipe they get erinmore or con-
dor in the small tins, one I can slip in and out of my prison
jeans pocket. These tins are at a premium now, in prison, as
all tobacco seems to come in plastic pouches. Being
biodegradable they dry and split before long.

Well now I'v got the embarrassing, beggin bit over.

I arrived at Blundeston with 5 tee shirts, and was only
allowed 2. blundeston also would not allow me my track suit
bottoms. At this place I'm allowed all 5 tee shirts, and the
bottoms.

At Blundeston I was allowed to purchase a gas disposable
cigarette lighter for £1.50. Here it was confiscated.

I have been allowed varnish in every prison I'v been in.
Here a brand new tin is confiscated.

We are allowed to go down for assosiation for 2 hours
every evening. If we don't go down we are locked in our
cells, for the 2 hours. We are not allowed to visit each others
cells. That's not a bad thing, as most of the cuttings and stabbings happen during the assoseation.

The cons here are not a bad lot, and seem at ease with each other.

I wrote to the No 1 Governor at Wandsworth and the Minister for prisons, about the screws at Wandsworth getting red in the face and spraying spittle in the face of a young remand prisoner just for haveing a hand in his pocket.

I got the same treatment the next day for having my hands in my pockets. I haven't had anyone scream at me since I did my national service.

They, the screws at wandsworth, are cowards and bullies. There seems to be a click of screws at wandsworth, and other local nicks that vie with each other to see how many cons they goad into earning them selfs a kicking.

It's easy to be brave, when the touch of a button or the toot of a panic whistle can make you instantly mob handed, You can never lose a fight that way and these young hot headed screws know it and play on it.

The screws here so far are a easy going lot. No hestericle shouting. Kind words and easy going ways, just the way I like it.

No piss pots here. A large plastic bucket in which to pee, or shit. I feel like our willie in the Sunday post, only he is upside down.

On assoseation we have two TVs – one for video, one for whatever the toughest man in the room wants to watch. A pool table, mini, dart board, tennis table.

That's 9 prisons I'v been in. I wonder where those prisons are that have TVs in there cells. I'v heard that howard on about makeing life toughter for prisoners. Cons have already been captured. The crime is happening out there, not in here. Cons, conning each other, and all the trouble that entails yes; drug abuse yes; cell theaving yes; stabbings yes; cuttings yes; ganging up on some unfortunate and half killing him yes; burning someones cell out yes; heaving boiling liquid in someones face yes; building up large depts, and dissapering on the numbers yes; grassing each other up yes; bulling, yes; intimidating the vunerable yes; homosexual abuse of the vunerable yes; Other than that life is so, so peacefull!!

The lord gave man everything he needs, and more. Then he gave us arseholes to shit on it.

I'm going to spend some time with other mens flowers, a beautiful, beautiful book. More later,

P.S. I did read your letter in the news sheet, 'Nice'.

Well its later. I found a great disgarded book, just before I left Blund. A good housekeeping cookery book. I keep going back to it, especialy the chapters on cakes, puddings and biscuits. I will try to hang on to it for when and if I get out. Apple and blackberry charlotte, stuffed baked apples, rhubarb crumble, what stuff, Thats enough of that drooling.

If I look out of the cell window, I stare at a brick wall. If I cast my eyes down I see a small yard of garbage. To my right I see other cells To my left a ruddy great fence, topped with razor wire.

I got out to the sports field today for an hour, lovely huge field, bags of room.

It always surprises me, how few prisoners go out when they get the chance.

There's masses of grounds here, most of it is show ground, that means it is kept in good condition to show to V.I.P.s

If you came on an official visit you would be showen these grounds. If you noticed how much of it was worn by prisoners feet you would see how much is actully used by us. But I must be fair. This sports field is the biggest I'v seen in any prison I'v been to.

'More as it comes'

29-8-93

Breakfast:- 2 weetabix ½ pint pasturised milk, pint of prison diesel (tea), luke warm, and a pint of my own tea, two tea bags, sugar, milk from Breakfast nice and hot.

The milk comes from camp hill prison, ten minute walk from here. Parkhurst prison is on this Island too.

Exersise at 9-45 till 11-15. Sports field, goody.

'later'

When I was in Swaleside, I made a clay ash tray, which I used in my last three nicks with no problems. Here it is confiscated.

When I left maidstone, a young prison officer, Andy, gave me a ninja turtle mug, which I used even on the seg in blundeston. Here it is confiscated.

So you see the vagaries from prison to prison. That young officer, Andy, said I was the quietest con, and the only one he had ever met he could call a gentleman, 'So I can't be all bad',

7.13PM Sunday

If you walked into this prison through the front gate you would be amazed at the flower and plant display, dozens of massive flower beds, in full bloom, and wonderfull colours.

We cons see them as we arrive, and dont see them again, till we leave. Again, these are just for show, for V.I.P. visitors. If you then walk towards the back of the prison where the wings are, you would see the prison proper. Austerity is the word. Dull brick, huge fences, and bundles of razor wire. 'Aint life a gas.'

I have not started personalising my cell yet. I'll wait till my induction period is over, to see what plans they have for me here. 'A job I hope'

I got £2.50 advance, ¾ of old holborn, £1.66 per ½ oz 83p per ¼ oz 1p left till next week.

The advance has to be paid back at 50p per week, So I will get £2, per week till its paid. Lucky I had some rizlas with me.

Here goes this mad pen again. I hope you don't get browned off with all this stuff.

I had to put my taste buds on hold, by laying aside my cook book.

I don't know what it is about prison food. You eat it, and about an hour later you almost achieve lift off, every twenty minutes or so. Or you belch so much you almost bowl over the person in front of you. If the cooks an Arab, hell be well pleased.

I was very interested, in your friend who spent 3 years in solitary. It is amazing how some individuals can endure.

I hope you come across a thin paper back TOUCHING THE VOID. I think with your army background you would understand the courage involved. It's a gut wrenching story.

Your sentence, like speaking to sailors traped in a sunken submarine – 'It says it all.' It's lovely

Well I better let you have this one
and save some for another time

Yours Aye
T Shannon
TOM

P.S. anything to fill in a space,
P.P.S. It's filled.
   What's happening at the Pond?

c/o Prison Reform Trust
59 Caledonian Road
N1 9BU

5th September 1993

Dear Tom,

How wonderful to get a long cheerful letter from you, full of optimism and interest in life again – quite like old times. Perhaps things have come full cycle since we started writing and you seemed to have your life fairly well organised and to your liking at Maidstone. I do hope so and that things go on at Albany the way they've started. Let us hope too that you never, ever spend 9 weeks in the seg again.

I'm afraid I don't have a tobacco tin – only an old Manikin cigar tin which you can have if you think it will help. I'll keep my eyes out for a better one but it's years since we did away with tins. Sorry!

Isn't it amazing how different gaols interpret the rules differently. There seems to be no reason behind it. Totally baffling. Perhaps it makes someone somewhere feel important to impose a restriction. It would be interesting if you were to set down your memories of each of all the gaols you've been in. It could go in the book as a sort of alternative Tumim Report.

What do you mean by 'disappearing on the numbers'? Also, you talk about cons 'grassing each other up'. I thought grassing was something no con would do – not just out of honour but out of self-preservation too. Please enlighten me.

Yes, I did read 'Touching the Void'. It is an incredible story, isn't it. Such guts! But I felt sorry for the guy who cut the rope. He's made to look a shit but what else could he do? I didn't much like the author but I do admire him. It's an enthralling read.

What's our news? Not much. We've been spraying the stubbles, spreading dung and trimming the hedges. We do the hedges with one of those flail things [I say 'we' but I mean Peter does them. I'll pity the hedge that I ever have a go at!] People criticize these machines as brutal but if you do it every year, you finish up with a very neat, thick hedge. They only look ravaged when they've been left too long and the wood has got too thick. Anyway, there's no time to do them by hand as in the old days. Next, we'll start the Autumn ploughing and sowing – less of it this year as we're into set-aside.

Some of our grass snake's eggs have hatched – the ones in the hot cupboard. Now, we've got four minute grass snakes, perfect in every detail but no bigger than shoe-laces. Whatever can we find them to eat that will be small enough? If we can't solve this, we'll set them free. It seems a daft system for snakes to hatch out in early September when the tadpoles are too big for them to eat and winter lies ahead. None of the snakes we ever had seemed very bright.

Now that things have started in such a good way at Albany, I do hope you'll be able to keep them that way. The screws seem to want to treat you with respect. If you can reciprocate, even to the ones in the POA, perhaps you will enter into a virtuous circle in which things get better and better until, one fine day, you are free again. I do hope so.

Yours ever,
Chris

PS I enclose an article which may interest you.
PPS Did I ever tell you, we've started horse breeding (mainly because I've got an old mare and I don't know what else to do with her. She's got something wrong in her back which makes her a bit unpredictable to ride.) Her first foal is due next May. I hope there isn't a horse mountain in the EEC by then.

Dear Chriss

It must be our first year's anniversary of writing to each other, because classic F.M. are celebrating there first birthday. It was just about the time they came on the radio that we started writing. If so, the year has gone quick, in some ways, and dragged in others.

I did get the three tapes you sent. Lovely stuff. I was not allowed to have the battries. We are not allowed to have batteries sent in here, but I got them after a fuss. A young officer got them for me, and told me to tell my wife, not to send any more. 'So there you go misses. Don't send any more battries.'

Thanks to your kindness, I now have eight tapes, a good little collection. I keep my tapes, and my walkman tucked out of sight, not because of cell thives, but to deter borrowers. Cons, somehow seem to damage stuff you lend to them, or you can get into a right bull and cow, trying to get stuff back.

Did you here the con who was released from wymot prison just before the riot, He told the reporter all I'v been saying to you. The gangster culture, drug baron's, bullies, and drug abusers, male rape.

It is said, that sucide, or attemted sucide are crys for help. I wonder how many of the cons who took part in that riot, did so, knowing that they would be moved out of that prison. The drug barons, and the bullies, or the tax collectors, would not want a riot. They have everything the way they want it.

Those so called key prisons, the con has a key to his own door. He can lock his cell when he goes to work or to fetch his meal. 'BUT' when he is in his cell, he can't lock himself in, or some of them would lock them selfs in and refuse to come out even for food. Then the pressure jack would have to be used, to blast the door off its hinges.

The only secure peace, and security, any con can have, is the security of being banged up, out of reach, of bullies and perverts. I have read storries of old warriors, where they can fall asleep in any conditions, and be instantly awake, even, at the sound of an insect alighting on a leaf.

Can you imagine how it must be for a soft youngster, not knowing what will come through his cell door next, the horror, the terrible horror. The sheer mind blowing, cut wrenching debilitating exhaustive existence. Fuck it, fuck it, fuck it. The you'll do's are the ones who get the worse of it.

Ah well. What the hell will my writing about it do. 'Zut Alors'

I wonder if Judge Tumin will have the balls to lay the blame, at the feet of the P.O.A. and its members, or will the P.O.A. come off lily white again.

The numbers means protection. There is a rule:- 'Rule 43'. You can ask to go on rule 43, BUT you would have to give the names. Who are you afraid of? And why? Or to put it another way, 'Grass someone up'.

Debt builders, 'at least some of them', arrive at a prison, the first thing they find out is who the main dealers are. Then, useing there own methods – flannel, flattery, bullshit, – they build up sometimes enormous debts. Then one day they are not on the wing. They put themselfs on 43, or on numbers, or on the rule.

They, the (professional dept builders) have been known to cut themselfs, just to show something, to justify there fear, and desperate need for protection. They grass one or two minor barons. They are then goasted to another nick, laughing all the way. ITS TRUE, I love them. To see the disgusting barons crying in there drinking chocolate, warms the cockles of my ticker.

'Now', there are young idiots, who get into dept, then find them selfs being threatened or abused. Fear, or advice from someone like me makes them go to the wing SO, or FO, who, puts them on numbers for there own protection. I don't need protection. I have a reputation as an utter, utter, nutter. I'm given a wide berth.

'No one Grasses anyone up in jail?' you say, or thought.

(Long time later.) Sorry I'v been away so long, I was rolling on the floor laughing my nuts off!! There's more grasses, in the criminal fraternity, than you have blades of grass on your farm.

Winson Green, B'ham, Wormwood Scrubs, london, Swaleside, Kent. Pentonville London, Scrubs again, 1 month. Long Lartin midlands, Maidstone Kent, Blundeston, where? Wondsworth 2 nights 1 day. Albany Isle of Wight, That's all the prisons I'v been in. I will take them one at a time, and write my report on each in future letters, starting with the one after this.

I started a brick course today. My wrist is so painful, as for my back. 'God help me' It will take a few weeks to get used to work again.

Chriss, thank you for trying to find a tin for me. I don't think I will need one now, as I think I'v stopped smokeing. At least I did not buy any tobaco last saturday, and my order for this week has already gone in again no tobaco. I hope I can keep it up. It's torture. I'll try hard.

I had a terrible letter from the social services in the U.S.A. Cindy my x wife has abandoned my boys again. The S.S. found out they have been badly treated. Now Debra, Cindy's sister has the boys on her ranch. The boys are temporary wards of Mucomb County Court.

I'm haveing to leave it to Jean to deal with it. All I can do is blank it out. If I let it in, god help me. I know Anson, Cindys husband. He will see me again.

So you did read Touching the Void. You can't help, but feel

for the one who cut the roap. Bone mends, pain is forgotten, that knife will always be in that lads hand.

I found my thesaurus. It has no covers, and the legend on the first page in orange ink is;- this book is shit. God knows what the fool who took it thought he was stealing. Perhaps with it being so well used and worn, he thought he was getting an old and well loved cunt book. What a dissapointment it must have been for him.

Most of the books in the decrepit condition of my thesaurus are well handled cunt books that do the rounds for ever. Some of them have been in prison for longer than any human. I would not touch one of these books with a barge pole, not that I'm a prude. It's just that a descent hard on could prove fatal for my present condition!!

I don't know why I'm excited about the horse breeding, but I am. I remember some gypsies near us. I was always with the horses. Other boys were chased away from them. Why don't you chase him one boy said pointing at me. The gypsy said;- 'He's a horse boy. We know horse boys.' Roll on may. You must have your camera ready when the foul stands. Great stuff.

The article you said you enclosed, wasen't in the envelope.

I'v been told I can only write so many pages as it makes the letter too heavy, and over a certain weight it's classed as a package. Are they having me on?*

Any books you have finished with, and wish to send to me will always be welcome. I can't help thinking of the postage all this costs you.

As for my varnish, the tin is kept in the wing office. I can have it between 6–8 in the evening. 'Gods truth.'

This week I ordered my £4.80 wages. Steradent 90p Marvel 1.36p Sacharin 90p tea bags 30p for twenty, Wine gums 24p 'No tobacco,'

---

*I once weighed one of Tom's longer letters of three pages. It was 15 grams. The GPO's limit for ordinary letters is 60 grams.

Well I'm off to bed to help classic F.M. celebrate there birthday. It's a pity we are not allowed to take part in there phone or postal competitions. I should have liked to have won one of there classic F.M. sweatshirts.

A farmer, at the cattle show, washing the belly of his prize bull.

A young man asks the farmer;- 'What time is it sir?'

The farmer touches the bulls balls. 'It's 10 past two,' he says. The young man is amazed, goes and gets his friend. 'What time is it, sir?' The farmer touches the bull balls. '20 past two,' he says. The young man gives the farmer a $50 note. 'Show me how you do that, sir.' The farmer puts the note in his pocket. 'Sit on this stool,' he says. 'Move the bulls balls to your right. See that clock back there!!'

Good bye till again,
T Shannon
TOM

c/o Prison Reform Trust
59 Caledonian Road
N1 9BU

17th September 1993

Dear Tom,

You must forgive me for not replying at once to your 'anniversary' letter. I didn't reply at once because I wanted to do it justice. It is so full of interest but its arrival coincided with the start of my annual wrestling match with the farm accounts. I can't complete them of course till the farm-year ends (30 Sep), but I like to get the entries up to date and balanced. In theory, it only takes a morning.

One of my great dreams is to prove that theory. It always actually takes me about two days and nights. I achieve this by building in some minute error so that when I've finished, the figures don't quite balance. The rest of the time is spent trying to find the error. This time it was a transposition problem. I had copied £153.50 as £135.50 and, while everything balanced within the computer, it did not agree with the bank balance. I'm afraid this letter had to wait while the hunt was on.

First of all, I want to say how appalled I am by the news from your boys. I had hoped that you could at least have a quiet mind on their account. I remember, you did not want them to know that you were in prison. I wonder how much that matters now. If their mother and step-father have abandoned them (which actually seems a good thing), everyone else will need to rally round to fill the gap. Let us hope that Debra can fill some of it – but could you not help her? It would surely help her and them if they knew you cared, even though you couldn't do much materially.

You may think I am being nosey. I know nearly nothing of

your family and have no right to offer advice, but I don't think you should hide yourself because of the crime you committed. I don't know much about that either and am not asking to be told, but such a thing can happen almost by accident – and what's done cannot be undone. It does not sound to me like the crime of a habitual criminal. I can't believe your boys would reject you because of it. You can't help them materially, having no material, but you could help them a lot morally – even if it's only to teach them what a hell-hole is a gaol. But just to take an interest in them could mean a lot to them. Remember how you resent your father for ignoring you and Michael.

Furthermore, I think your boys could help you, giving you a purpose in life and adding to your value and self-esteem. I do hope therefore that you will <u>not</u> leave it all to Jean as you say in your letter. I hope that you will take this chance to become for them the best father you are allowed to be.

Enough – sermon over. Sorry about that but it got me quite steamed up to think of your boys suffering, as you and Michael did.

I read and re-read your letter many times. What an upside down world prison is. How little the world outside understands it. I would have assumed (as the designers must have done) that to give cons the key to their cell would have been a comfort and a privilege. It never occurred to me that it spelt danger. The extraordinary thing is that it would be so easy to design the fault out, giving the screws an over-riding key. Every hotel manager has one.

Reading your letters about the bullying, the violence, the drugs, the fear and all the horrors of prison life, leaving aside the behaviour of some of the screws, and then reading in the papers about our gaols being too soft, I wonder what connects the two. Are they both about the same subject? This is one reason why I would like to find a publisher for your letters. I think they <u>ought</u> to be read. (Incidentally, here is the article I forgot to send with my last letter.)

Talking of publication, I have a feeling that we might have reached a good moment to close the book. A year has passed, amazing things have happened – the Stanley knife and the spinach sandwich, the stabbing, the shitty cell and the hunger strike, the three months in seg – and now, at last, you seem to have reached calmer waters again. Furthermore, there is just the possibility that a whole new family dimension is about to open up in your life. I hope so and I hope that it will make your life better and more purposeful. But I think it is something for volume 2.

So I propose to draw the line here on the book but not, I hope, on our correspondence. I hope we will keep that going as long as it helps you and me to make sense of our lives and of the world we live in.

Yours ever,
Chris

EPILOGUE

Tom's exhilaration on arrival at Albany did not last long. His confrontation with the authorities at Blundeston had sapped his vitality. In addition, he now had family problems to contend with.

His ex-wife Cindy and her new man, accused of abusing the two boys, had abandoned them. The American Social Services decided that they should be adopted, and required Tom to renounce his rights and responsibilities as their natural father. He could hardly refuse, but it cost him dear for he has always blamed his own spoiled life on his father's abandonment of the family. He feared the boys would be lost to him and perhaps to each other. His great hope was that their aunt, Debra, would adopt them, and he wrote to her and to them about his wishes and concerns.

Months passed without any response until, to relieve the tension, Jean, his Probation Officer, rang her opposite number and learned that they were living happily with Debra, had received his letters and would have written if they could have thought of anything to say. Of such stuff is agony made.

In November, the enlightened governors of Albany organized a Lifers' Families Day to which Tom invited Jean and

Ann and me. We went and spent the day in the prison chapel, hearing lectures and chatting together. Tom is a small wiry man, with bright eyes and a neat black beard – at least it was neat that day. He looked younger than his years which he says is common with prisoners, for whom time is standing still. He took immense pains to make us enjoy our day, explaining everything and introducing us to other cons, especially to those who had no visitors. He seemed to be friends with everyone, exchanging well-worn jokes and banter with one and all. We came away feeling that the day had been a success for him, and it certainly was for us.

This was a relief but I still feared that an invisible crying tree, once seen, might lose its efficacy. For a while, I thought it had. Tom's letters became shorter, less vivid and less poetic, but this was temporary. Now, three years and two more prisons later, we still write weekly and our friendship is as strong as ever. Happily there have been no more fights or hunger strikes, no more seg or even adjudications. Much credit for this must go to the staff at Albany who first treated him with respect.

Our letters are about other things – his family in America, this book and the hope that he may soon be on the count-down to release. They are no less entertaining than they used to be. I do not think he regrets the dramas of the bad old days but he recently wrote that 'things here are so quiet I get excited when a butterfly flaps its wings.'

September 1996